The Challenge of the Digital Economy

Francesco Boccia • Robert Leonardi
Editors

The Challenge of the Digital Economy

Markets, Taxation and Appropriate Economic Models

palgrave
macmillan

Editors
Francesco Boccia
President Standing Committee of the Budget
Italian Chamber of Deputies
Rome, Italy

Robert Leonardi
LUISS University
Rome, Italy

ISBN 978-3-319-43689-0 ISBN 978-3-319-43690-6 (eBook)
DOI 10.1007/978-3-319-43690-6

Library of Congress Control Number: 2016957774

Printed on acid-free paper

This Palgrave Macmillan imprint is published by Springer Nature
The registered company is Springer International Publishing AG
The registered company address is Gewerbestrasse 11, 6330 Cham, Switzerland

This book is dedicated to Edouardo, Ludovica, Gea and Isabella who were born once the digital revolution was already under way and whose lives will be touched by all aspects of it. We would also like to acknowledge the support received by our respective wives, Nunzia and Raffaella, who have steadfastly provided encouragement in the preparation of this book and in our research in general.

Preface

The biggest error we could commit is to face the ongoing digital revolution divided into hermetically sealed compartments: the industrialists by themselves, so too the trade unions, the musicians and actors on one side and the journalists on the other, the athletes by themselves along with the young bloggers who maintain that they do not need rules as if royalties and copyrights were only important to some authors and not to others, in addition to doctors, teachers at different levels and shopkeepers. It is evident that the issue of the digital economy is not only a question of culture but also one of politics in the sense of being able to formulate effective policies that do not separate the collective interest from the common good but are able to focus on the instruments necessary for its achievement.

Equality, ethics and redistribution cannot be considered alternative values. They remain the founding principles of a modern society. The digital economy can be conceived as a compass so that we do not get lost in exploring the new worlds that have emerged. We now face an epoch-making revolution that is comparable than that of the discovery of the wheel, sail or paper. Certainly it is bigger in terms of its economic impact to those that brought about the industrial revolution: from the steam engine to electricity, and from mechanization to the first computers.

With the wheel we began to move objects around, with the sail we crossed the sea, and with paper we found out what was around the corner or what happened before our time. Now, with digital highways the world is in constant movement and we know everything about everyone. Is this not a revolution? Of course it is, but as with the wheel, sail, paper or electrical energy it needs to be managed, and to do this we need to recognize and understand it. And that is what this volume attempts to do: understand the nature of the revolution, analyse the proposals that have been made to manage it, and suggest the basic steps that need to be undertaken in order to render the revolution a positive change rather than a destructive one. Both outcomes are possible and we need to act quickly to make sure that the positive course of action is the one we choose.

Francesco Boccia

Acknowledgements

We would like to thank the staff of the Standing Committee on the Budget of the Italian Chamber of Deputies and of the Research Office of the Chamber. Particular thanks goes to Antonio Illacqua, legal advisor to the Committee, who helped in the preparation of the first "web tax" proposal presented to the Chamber in 2013, and to Ermanna Sarullo who provided the crucial coordination in bringing this volume to completion.

Contents

Biographies

Salvatore Biasco is Professor of International Monetary Economics at the Sapienza University in Rome and former Chairperson in the XIII Legislature of the Bicameral Committee for Fiscal Reform on the Italian Parliament. He has written a series of books on the political culture of the Left in Italy, including *Regole, stato, uguaglianza: La posta in gioco nella cultura della sinistra e nel nuovo capitalismo* (2016).

Francesco Boccia was nominated President of the Italian Chamber of Deputies' Standing Committee on Budget and Finance in April 2013 and has been serving in that capacity ever since. He has been a member of Parliament since 2008. Before being elected to Parliament he served as Professor of Territorial Economics at the Carlo Cattaneo University Castellanza (Varese, Italy) since 2000. He spent four years at the London School of Economics and an extended period doing research at the University of Illinois at Chicago. From 2016 he has been President of the Research Centre on Governance and Public Policy at the University of Molise where he teaches Public Administration.

Robert Leonardi is Professor of Political Science at the LUISS University in Rome in the Department of Political Science and the School of Government. Between 1991 and 2010 he taught at the London School of Economics in the Department of Government and the European Institute. He is author of a number of ground-breaking volumes on the Cohesion Policy of the European Union. He was part of the team led by Robert Putnam at Harvard University which defined and elaborated the role of social capital as an essential element in determining the institutional performance of regional and local governments

Michael A. Pagano is Dean of the College of Urban Planning and Public Affairs at the University of Illinois at Chicago (UIC), professor of public administration, elected Fellow of the US National Academy of Public Administration and Faculty Fellow of UIC's Great Cities Institute. He is the co-editor of the *Urban Affairs Review* (2001–2014) and the 2011 recipient of the Daniel Elazar Distinguished Scholar Award of the American Political Science Association (APSA). He is the author of six books, including *The Dynamics of Federalism in National and Supranational Political Systems* (2007), *Metropolitan Resilience in a Time of Economic Turmoil* (2014), *Citiscapes and Capital* (1995), and *Terra Incognita: Vacant Land and Urban Strategies* (2004). He is currently the Principal Investigator of a multiyear John D. and Catherine T. MacArthur Foundation-funded research project on city fiscal behaviour and financial adaptations during the Great Recession.

Raffaele Russo is Head of the Base Erosion and Profit Shifting (BEPS) Organisation for Economic Co- operation and Development (OECD) study carried out by the OECD Centre for Tax Policy and Administration. Before joining the OECD he was Senior Associate of the International Tax Academy in Amsterdam. He is the author of *The Attribution of Profits to Permanent Establishment* (2005) and *Fundamentals of International Tax Planning* (2007).

Antonio Uricchio is Rector of the University of Bari and chair of Fiscal Law. He has taught in a number of universities in Latin America (Uruguay and Argentina) and in Europe. He has contributed articles to the leading journals in fiscal law in Italian and international journals.

List of Figures

List of Table

1

Introduction: The Digital Economy and Fiscal Policy in the Age of E-Commerce

Francesco Boccia

1.1 The Issues to Be Discussed and the Alternatives That Are Available

The extraordinary importance of the digital economy to businesses, services and to the production of value in various sectors of the economy has not always been clear for all to see. The intense debate in the Italian parliament, the European Commission's Report, the OECD BPES working group, and the debate in several states in the USA testify to how much society has changed in the era of the digital economy and so must the tax regime that regulates relations between governments, service companies, and industrial enterprises. Such a complex issue must be approached with the clarity, determination and rigour typical of the analysis of economic phenomena. The USA, France, Germany, UK, Spain and most of the European governments are moving in the same direction as Italy: those

F. Boccia (✉)
President of Standing Committee on the Budget, Italian Chamber of Deputies, Rome, Italy

F. Boccia, R. Leonardi (eds.), *The Challenge of the Digital Economy*,
DOI 10.1007/978-3-319-43690-6_1

who produce profits in a country should pay taxes in that same country. Most of the chapters presented in this volume were initially delivered by the authors at the Interparliamentary Conference under Article 13 of the Fiscal Compact held in the Chamber of Deputies in Rome as part of the 2014 Italian Presidency of the European Union.

After an introductory discussion of the issues associated with e-commerce and the questions that have been raised regarding national tax regime and how taxation is applied to the multinational corporations operating on the Web, this book looks at the wider international debate. Does it make sense to impose one uniform approach on companies operating on the Web or should each large market (e.g., the USA, the European Union (EU) and China) have their own separate taxation rules? This question is important in that the Web is universal in nature, and the profits that are generated flow to a limited number of operators who have established their dominant presence in the world market.

The volume consists of eight chapters that cover the ongoing debate from a theoretical as well as a legal point of view in addition to looking at specific cases of how the Internet has affected commerce and the impact that cross-border interactions have had on the tax base in important national markets. We wind up the volume with the Appendix which summarizes the work carried out by the European Commission in support of the BPES initiative undertaken by the OECD in response to the 2012 mandate to formulate recommendations on how to reform the rules for international tax regimes to make them capable of tackling the issues and opportunities presented by the expanding digital economy and increased cross-border transactions undertaken by multinational corporations.

In the discussion on the tax policies implemented by the large multinational corporations that dominate the Internet, we are referring to large Web multinationals, such as Google, Facebook, Amazon, AirBnB, Apple, eBay, Baidu, JD.com, Alibaba, Netflix, Samsung and a few others that, under the current conditions, continue to enjoy tax privileges not available to others. With the arrival of the digital economy, the value chain has been deeply and radically changed and the dematerialization of the generation of wealth requires a totally reformed tax system, otherwise we will simply continue to fuel a bad example of unfair competition to the detriment of national financial interests and the overall health of

Europe's economy. It is no longer acceptable to allow foreign companies to pay taxes in the countries where they have their registered office (obviously with a considerably cheaper tax rate) rather than in those where they operate with production and sales activities. The issue primarily concerns the huge market for the sale of goods and services online and the purchase of so-called search advertising, the advertising spaces that appear on the pages of search engines, and secondly, all activities related to online services (music, cinema, tourism and games, to name a few) and the entire sector of electronic commerce (e-commerce). This is the idea of the proposal that, in 2013, was brought to the attention of the Italian Parliament and the European political and cultural debate.

Paying a tax to the country where the company is generating profits is, moreover, in line with the general principle of similar proposals in other European countries. It also meets the severe difficulties of operators that maintain their headquarters in the EU. The point is not to increase the tax burden, but to create equal rules for all. The debate that has been raging about what was wrongly and provocatively renamed the "web tax," "Google tax," and "Amazon tax" demonstrates how poorly the issue is understood. This is an issue that is much broader than the digital economy and that is often limited to superficial considerations. The so-called web tax does not restrict access to the network and is not against those who surf the net, but it is aimed at those who do not pay taxes in the countries in which they operate and therefore are in a position to remove billions of euros and dollars (and therefore also jobs) from the domestic market. It is not a new tax for the citizens but an attempt to equalize from a tax perspective the taxes paid by multinationals that are operating on the Internet and are enjoying huge tax breaks.

It is unthinkable that, today, in the world of the digital economy a company pays tax only in the country where it has its registered office. A company must pay "indirect" taxes on sales and part of its "direct" taxes in the country in which it produces, sells and generates its profits. The entire digital economy is worth almost 22% of world gross domestic product (GDP) and is growing at an unprecedented rate. And it is absurd that with such growth national governments only manage to pick up the crumbs. We are not talking therefore about increasing taxation but creating equal rules for everyone. This would allow us, among other things, to trace cash flows that are fleeing abroad. The web tax that has been under so much discussion in recent years is anything but a tax. It merely states that companies that do business in Italy should charge Italian value-added tax (VAT) rates, just as, in France, the French use the national VAT and likewise other countries apply their own national rates, with the same being true in the case of the 50 US states where sales taxes are collected at the local level.

There is no new tax in Italy that is aimed at hitting the web multinationals; the aim is to apply the same VAT rate that Italian businesses pay today in Milan or Bari no matter where the companies have their headquarters or where they earn their profits. Taxation then, for the digital economy, must be entirely switched to indirect taxes in the form of the so-called "consumption taxes" that are represented by the sales taxes in the USA or the VAT levies in Europe. This was exactly the solution proposed by the Italian Parliament in 2013. The proposal that was the subject of parliamentary debate was in line with European regulations. The aim was to oblige the client, if they were taxable, to purchase from a company possessing an Italian VAT code. No obligatory opening of a VAT number by taxable subjects in non-European countries was envisaged. The taxation, among other things, did not clash either with the European Directive of November 2006 or with the Italian legislative decree of 2010 that transposes the provisions of the Directive into Italian law. That text, in fact, made it clear beyond any doubt, that "the provision of services is not applied in the territory of the State (the list also includes advertising services) when rendered to non-taxable clients."

The turbulence in the stock exchanges in addition to the highest share price in history (Alibaba), definitively contribute to the rewriting the boundaries of the commercial world. The celebrated "silk road" that historically connected East and West seems to have been reconfirmed. The USA and China compete but also intertwine themselves financially and commercially at the world level. They challenge each other by skipping traditional geographical boundaries, but through their competition they absorb the value produced by the smaller continental economies that emerged in the pre-Internet world. The USA in a de facto capacity and based on its technological superiority supervises the exchange of information on the net of much of the so-called Western world, largely exceeding the 1 billion consumers in the Americas, Europe including Russia, Oceania as well as large parts of Africa and Asia. Beijing has over 600 million Chinese on the Web and is able to reach 1 billion consumers including those outside its borders. Among today's top-ten Chinese billionaires, five belong to the Web. Globally, among the first ten web companies, six are US and four are Chinese.

The market capitalization of the top four US companies that do not strictly manufacture anything is 800 billion dollars (Google, Facebook, Amazon and eBay), not counting giants such as Apple in the business of smartphones and tablets; and 450 billion dollars for the Chinese companies (Alibaba, Baidu, Tencent and JD.com). These are impressive numbers not only for the businesses involved but also for the value that they produce. What we have to consider is how and to what extent do they aspire to control the wealth of other countries? They virtually do not pay taxes; their investments are only made where their headquarters are located; and they benefit from the use of offshore accounts to hide their profits from national tax authorities.

And what is happening in Europe? In the past it has been silent; it has not placed into question the rules that have allowed multinationals engaged in the digital economy to avoid taxes and even hide their profits in tax havens. However, during the last four years this situation has begun to change owing to the shift in national approaches to the taxation of the multinational companies that we have witnessed in the UK, France and Italy. The European Commission has also moved to change the rules, and at the world level there has been a focused attempt to close down tax havens that have permitted nationals of other countries to avoid the payment of taxes.

This book sets out to contribute to the discussion that does not just affect the value of the shares that may increase or decrease in the stock exchanges of Wall Street, London or Milan, but that has a considerable impact on the deconstruction taking place between the value of the services and goods provided, produced and marketed through the digital economy. All this is taking place in a world without borders and, we would add, without rules. There is no doubt that people's lives can change for the better through the use of information technology, but if that same technology alters the basic principles of fair taxation, we all risk feeling the prospect of being more modern but also more poor.

With a concentration of wealth and information never before seen in the history of world capitalism, I believe that finally putting in order a market of vast dimensions, which today contains strong elements of unfairness and injustice, must become a political priority. And there can be no negotiation; it comes down to deciding whether we are on the side of fairness or not. To the advocates of the Rome Treaty[1]—a Treaty that is historically defined—and the free movement of goods I would respond that the Internet and its revolution in the functioning of the economy is the successor to the same Treaty. It takes advantage of the Treaty but it does not abide by the rules of a fair return in relation to the payment of taxes on the profits generated, as is the case for every other firm doing business in Europe. Do we want to adapt to the times in terms of providing a level playing field for all of those who do business in the EU? What is at stake is not only what happens in Europe but what happens in the world. The actors involved are not only European; they span the entire spectrum of companies. Instead, what is at stake is the principle of fair competition and fair taxation. These two issues cannot be avoided. They need to be addressed in an open debate, and they need to be resolved in a manner that takes into account all of the interests involved. However, these decisions need to be taken quickly in order to avoid the negative consequences of the existing status quo.

1.2 Reflections on the Italian Experience

According to a check of the data, it is not strictly correct to say that the multinationals of the Web have not invested a euro in Italy, but in essence it is true. During the last Parliament when we had a centre-right government and were on the eve of passing the budgetary provisions (referred to in Italy as the "stability law") I was the coordinator of the economic

[1] The Rome Treaty was signed in 1957 and its objective was the creation of a Custom Union as the fundamental aspect of the Common Market. Since then the objectives of the European Union have moved on to include the creation of the single market provided for by the Single European Act (SEAT) of 1986. The single market set out to eliminate all of the non-tariff barriers to the free flow of goods, capital, services and people. The challenge posed by the digital economy is offered by multinational companies that have evaded both sales taxes (VAT) where they sell their goods and services and corporate tax where they make their profits through the use of "creative" tax avoidance schemes which are now the object of new legislation being introduced by the European Commission and member states.

committees of the Democratic Party. On that occasion, I proposed a change in the role of Società Italiana degli Autori ed Editori (SIAE),[2] the Italian copyright collection agency.

Thanks to this initial experience I began to focus on the difficulties of assessing the impact on the real economy of the distortions in the value chain introduced by the digital economy in different sectors. In some cases, through the introduction of innovations, the value chain has become shorter while in others it has completely distorted the market. In fact, the music industry has already changed radically. Out of that experience emerged the political-cultural debate that came out of the Chamber of Deputies in the subsequent legislature.[3] The year and a half of the Monti government, then, was a year of turbulence. It was difficult to put on the table issues of cultural relevance when the uppermost emergency was the state of the budget. So, despite my attempt at that time and the conviction of Pierluigi Bersani (the former head of the Democratic Party) to keep trying, we did not find a particularly fertile ground in advancing our proposals on the digital economy. Meanwhile, however, in that first part of this legislature (2013–present), relations with individual operators have intensified and, together with the Research Department of the Chamber of Deputies, we have widened the number of managers involved, the potential markets scrutinized and the understanding of how the rules have been functioning. If today in Italy there is some information, some data and a few numbers it is thanks to the excellent work that has been carried out within this context. I find it incredible in a country like Italy that until a little while ago it was the responsibility of a single academic to study what was happening. Professor Uricchio is the rector of the University of Bari and is one of the few scholars who has dealt with the issue of taxation of the Internet in his role as professor of tax law.[4] I found some of his articles in 2007 in international journals. Other articles have also appeared in scattered journals written by colleagues who had not worked together but

[2] SIAE is the Italian copyright collection agency that has enjoyed a monopoly position as the intermediary between the authors of music tracks and consumers. It was scheduled to be terminated on the basis of a vote of the European Parliament.

[3] I thank both Filippo Sugar and Gino Paoli, the current and former president of SIAE, for their participation in the continuous dialogue we have had over the past two years.

[4] Professor Uricchio's contribution is presented in Chap. 6 of this volume.

who had brought forward similar concerns. This fact struck not only me but also other parliamentary colleagues, such as Sergio Boccadutri, who joined the parliamentary debate in 2013 for the purpose of not trying to limit the Internet but rather to ensure that the real economy and the digital economy could work together and become one.

Why such a distinction exists I do not know, but in tax terms it exists. Companies operating in the real economy pay taxes and fees in the normal way; from a tax point of view the relationship between state and the operators in the field takes place according to the different rules in each country. Take Coca-Cola for example. In Europe a multinational corporation such as Coca-Cola uses 28 different VAT numbers in order to operate within each member state. In fact, any company that operates in Europe must have a VAT number for each country in which it is present. This is the same for an Italian company with offices and operations for the production and sale of its products in different countries in Europe.

This is not the case, however, for every business operating within the digital economy. The discussion with many colleagues in the Chamber of Deputies started from this point of departure, and we arrived at the definition of a tax structure related to those areas affected by the digital economy which has been referred to in the Italian debate as the "web tax." I prefer the definition offered by Carlo De Benedetti that maybe we should have called it a *freedom tax* to demonstrate that it was actually a tax that allowed the markets to operate freely. In reality, the so-called "web tax," is not a new tax, has never been so, nor was it ever intended to be. Instead, it is an attempt to link it to the VAT tax and to the payment of taxes by companies that operate in contexts in which VAT is already paid by other companies that are doing the same things but are based in Italy or in other individual European countries.

A company that does the same task as Google but was started in Italy by an Italian entrepreneur uses a VAT number not only if it provides support or offers other types of service but also if it sells advertising. The Budget Committee of the Chamber of Deputies voted unanimously for this form of legislation in December 2013; no parliamentary group voted against it. It is important for public opinion to be informed on the circumstances that took place when the bill was voted on in the Committee. Even if the legislation was passed late at night this could not be considered "a night raid." It went through on the basis of a unanimous vote. The day after, the media reacted in an exaggerated and uninformed manner. As a result, some of the parliamentary groups sought to reconsider their position. From that moment on the Five Star Movement, on the basis of the position staked out by Beppe Grillo, declared itself to be completely opposed to the web tax. There were also some problems within the Democratic Party in terms of understanding the nature of the phenomenon and explaining what needed to be done.

It is true that to say "they haven't paid a euro in tax" is misleading, but the amount actually paid in taxes was 6 million euros. Given the volume of the turnover in sales, 6 million euros in taxes is not much at all. With the new rule establishing the traceability of sales that was introduced with the Stability Law of 2014, those 6 million have become 137 million. It is still too little; it is much too little if we think that just one company is worth almost as much as the entire capitalization of the Milan stock exchange. Think of all of the companies that come to mind that have dominated the Italian economy in the past. Even at the time of the dominance of the "Seven Sisters" in the petroleum industry, the oil firms never received such favourable treatment. To quote Fedele Confalonieri, the head of Fininvest, in the past it was not possible that two, three, four, five CEOs of large multinational companies could calmly declare to the media of various European countries that "maybe next year we will invest 15, 20, 30 billion dollars off-shore" while at the same time not paying their fair share in taxes. Nothing like that has ever happened.

As a university professor I have to explain to my students that offshore investments do exist. I have to explain that there is money that a shareholder or a manager may invest offshore. If you say it was an Italian businessman, even someone famous, I think that you would find someone at their house the next morning asking what does it means "to invest tens of billions offshore" in order to avoid taxation. But no one is outraged today. I have found these assessments disturbing but even more disturbing, was the deafening silence of the world around us. For this reason, I think that during the European semester of the Italian presidency, the prime minister presented this as a priority not only because it concerned Italy but because it was a question of civil conduct for firms operating in Europe. The value chain has completely changed. A pertinent example is offered by the music industry.

In the music industry the traditional processes of production and distribution have been entirely eliminated. Perhaps it still exists for those who produce metal bolts or other products you can touch, but it certainly hasn't existed for six, seven or eight sectors which several research centres have estimated comprise a tax base of between 25 and 30 billion euros. But this is still too low a figure. One should also factor in online games that are often not controllable—a tax base that, in the UK, is worth more than 80 billion euros and in Germany and France represents 60 billion and 50 billion euros, respectively. Is it possible to live in a Europe with such huge tax bases that do not have the least idea of what tax responsibility should govern the relation between government and industry and between member states?

I conclude the chapter by adding an impressive piece of data on e-commerce that we don't talk about much but should make us stop and think: total sales in Europe amount to 305 billion euros. In Italy, sales in 2015 reached the figure of 16.6 billion with a growth vis-à-vis 2014 of 16 %.

The largest growth has taken place in the purchase of books, music and electronic media (+31 %), electronic consumer goods (+21 %), fashion (+19 %) and tourism (+14 %). These represents 4 % of all retail sales that took place in Italy during 2015.

And if we look again at the numbers in the technology market we discover data on growth that we had forgotten. Business economists have discovered too late that the value chain has changed. I hope, however, that in the scientific community of tax scholars and lawyers it is possible to take immediate note that within the context of the digital economy it is insufficient to tax goods only in the place where they are produced, but it is also necessary to take into consideration the places where they are sold, transferred and delivered. If we do not change this paradigm we will never be able to establish a balanced form of competition between national and international firms nor will we be able to meet the needs of those sectors that are disappearing.

This is why we need to connect the real economy to the digital one, and we cannot afford to disconnect it. The crisis of the traditional information and communications technology (ICT) sector linked to the mechanisms of the past with the men who set up and removed computers is there for all to see. The situation for ICT solutions is quite different. The change has come in the use of ICT software, with digital advertising and with everything that is in some way similar to the services that characterize the digital world. There are two potential paths that are going in opposite directions: one is losing and the other is making money. One has double-digit growth in revenues, while the other is declining at a precipitous rate.

In the report prepared by the Chamber of Deputies Research Department it is estimated that, in 2012, there was a growth in the purchase of tablets by 69.1 %, of smartphones of 38.9 %, of smart TVs of 31.9 %, and of the downloading of music of 29 %. By 2016, it is reported that the purchase of smartphones had levelled off but this happened in a context in which consumers have, on average, two smartphones each and in which the potential use of the smartphone technology has been extended to all types of applications from the regulation of cooking and heating in one's private dwelling to the entire range of financial transactions.

Some manufacturers say that the music industry is in crisis. Discography, perhaps, is in crisis in terms of the production of DVDs, but the ability to listen to music is certainly not in crisis, even with these mechanisms perhaps you listen to even more music than before. And even children start to listen to music at an earlier age, not to mention the use of e-books that has grown by 84.6 %. I would say to Fedele Confalonieri that it is not the case that people do not read anymore but they do so in different ways. If all this has led web marketing to grow by 1100 % between 2005 and 2015 there must be a reason.

1.3 Issues That Have Emerged from the Italian Debate

The debate that has taken place in the Italian Parliament has to a great extent been paralleled in other European countries. It is useful to discuss some of the key aspects in order to inform the more general debate on e-commerce and taxation on the basis of the latest data that have recently been made available.

1.3.1 E-Commerce

E-commerce represents a potential growth channel for the export of Italian products and could play a decisive role in promoting the internationalization of, specifically, micro firms. In 2015 the value of e-commerce in the world exceeded 1200 billion dollars, an increase of 25 %, in contrast with the negative dynamics of consumption recorded from the beginning of the economic and financial crisis. E-commerce is, for the countries of the EU, a major channel for the increase of its commercial potential thereby enabling companies to reach distant markets: online sales have risen 22 % to a value of about 305 billion euros.

Small "digitally advanced" Italian businesses state that they have achieved a quarter of their revenues by selling abroad thanks to the e-commerce channel. But most Italian small to medium-sized enterprises (SMEs) have so far been unable to exploit the enormous potential of this sales channel, mainly owing to an extremely low level of digitalization. In fact, although the proportion of people reached by asymmetric digital subscriber line (ADSL) broadband in 2014 was 97 % but the "penetration rate" or effective use was only 58 % of the population (compared with 80 % in France, 85 % in Germany, 88 % in the UK and 68 % in Spain), only 35 % of the SMEs were online via their own websites. The barriers reported by Italian SMEs were mainly regulatory and tax in nature due to the non-homogenization of the rules on e-commerce in Europe. However, there are also barriers as a result of cultural gaps characterizing the personnel in the companies and the lack of adequate and specific management skills on the part of the managers in the company.

The value of sales on Italian sites in 2014 amounted to nearly 17 billion euros, less than a fifth of that in the UK, about a quarter of that in Germany and less than half in France. In addition, 90 % of sales were transacted using credit cards or PayPal. The market concentration is high; the top-20 players in e-commerce accounted for 71 % and the first 50 for 89 %. Purchases on mobile sites have grown by 160 % compared to 2011, in figures almost equal to 190 million euros.

1.3.2 The Markets Related to the Digital Economy

Survey data from the Italian Association for Information Technology (Assinform) confirm that in the face of a real economy that in 2012 grew at the global level by 3.2 % over the previous year, growth in the digital economy, defined as Digital Market, sped up at 5.2 %, reaching the level of almost 6 % of world GDP. In Europe, the average growth rate of GDP stood at 0.6 %, but the weight of the digital economy came to 6.8 % of European GDP.

This trend, although less dynamic than in the previous year (−2.1 % in 2011/10), signals the crisis of traditional ICT services (−4.7 %), representing more than half the value of the market, compared with the growth of the digital content and advertising (+7.2 %) and the software and ICT solutions (+2.4 %). The pressure of technological change is producing positive effects on segments related to the Web and to the mobile market: tablets at +69.1 %, smartphones at +38.9 %, smart TVs at +31.9 %, Internet at +18 %, Internet and eReader at +16.5 % (of which contents 7.2 % of which e-books +84.6 %, +29 % music, online publishing +13.4 %, software and application solutions +2.4 %.).

These segments were not affected by the crisis, but they were already present in the Italian economy by an average of 7.5 % and contributed to significant changes in consumption patterns and business growth. In decline, however, is turnover in the ICT industry that, for the fifth consecutive year, closed its accounts in the red with −4 %, related to turnover that was pushed down by the crisis of the traditional components. This still represents the bulk of the market. Estimates for 2014 of the Global Digital Market are −3.6 %, with traditional ICT at −5.8 %. This has serious repercussions on employment, especially being a labour-intensive industry which currently employs about 400,000 people.

In Italy the real economy in 2012 fell by −2.4 %, while the digital market, which represents 4.9 % of the national GDP, with a value of 68.141 billion euros, recorded a trend of −1.8 %. This trend, although less dynamic than in previous years (−2.1 % in 2011/10), signals the crisis of traditional ICT services (−4.7 %), which represent more than half the value of the market, compared with the growth of digital content and advertising (+7.2 %) and the software and ICT solutions sector (+2.4 %).

1.3.3 Sales Channels in Tourism

One out of two businesses offering accommodation has agreements with tourist intermediaries in marketing their offer to 58 % of hotels and 42 % of complementary structures. The Italian tourist industry relies on a mixture of traditional and web channels: 74 % of facilities (hotel and non-hotels) that rely on trade are present on the major online booking portals (e.g., Expedia, Opodo, Trivago, Bookings.Com, AirBnB and so on); 33 % choose to book through a tour operator; 35 % make their offerings through traditional travel agents; and 23 % through online travel agencies.

The Internet is used by Italian tourist businesses for multiple purposes—from promotion to marketing, and from customer satisfaction to spreading their reputation in Italy and abroad. It is a tool, however, that is beyond simple online presentation and not all operators fully exploit this option: 88 % of the structures own a site (92 % of hotels and 84 % of non-hotel) but the percentage drops to 29 % if we consider only those structures that have a website optimized for mobile browsing or that offer the ability to download applications directly onto smartphones; 64 % of companies offer the possibility of making the booking directly online through sites that are self-owned or through industry portals; 42 % of businesses are present on social networks (50 % of hotels and 36 % of the businesses outside of the hotels); 62 % of the operators regularly check the reviews left by customers on blogs, portals review (e.g., TripAdvisor) and Online travel agencies OTA (e.g., booking).

The advantage in terms of the sale of reservations was also confirmed in 2012, especially during the low season; businesses which make use of commercial intermediaries as well as those that allow for direct bookings online sell, on average, one room out of ten in the spring and autumn while during the year they have one booking more than other accommodation facilities. Increased use of the dual channels of websites and portals in the share of organized tourism brought the total to 16 % of the clientele for accomodation facilities in 2012 versus 11 % during the previous year, but also that of the tourists who book through the Internet ((53 % in 2014 vis-a-vis 47 % in 2012 and 41 % in 2011) 47 % of customers in 2012, 41 % in 2011). In particular, reservations made directly through the Web are growing, through the facility's site (19 % of customers in 2014; 11 % in previous years) or through the purchase from large portals and online booking (from 8 % to 12 % of customers).

Using the Internet are mainly tourists who choose to stay in the Italian art cities (52 % of customers, in particular 18 % through the website and

16 % through portals).[5] Then, there are the tourists who stay at facilities by the lakes or by the sea, destinations with accommodation structures where almost half of the customers book through the Internet: 19–22 % of customers by email, 15–17 % on the site of the structure and 13–14 % through major online portals.

1.3.4 Online Advertising

The results of the first study published by the Observatory on Advertising that is part of the Italian Communications Authority (AGCOM or Autorità per le garanzie nelle telecommunicazioni) are quite enlightening. The body analyses trends and transfers by separating above-the-line advertising (television, periodicals, films, radio, books, Internet, newspapers and billboards) from below-the-line advertising (direct marketing, sponsorship, web marketing, events, promotions and public relations (PR)). The survey, conducted between 1 February and 2 March 2012, involved about 1516 companies and various professionals. The data obtained are for the years 2010–2011. The Authority has dedicated a specific study to Communication on the Web (Sect. 1.3). According to the Observatory, since 2005, advertising in traditional media was reduced in favour of online, which grew by more than 1000 %, and investment in web marketing exceeds 3 billion euros. In 2011, the turnover for above-the-line advertising was 9.7 billion euros.

After an initial period of growth, since 2009 there has been a contraction in traditional media (newspapers, television and radio) which has not yet abated. Television has seen a fairly stable evolution over time; radio declined drastically in 2011, together with the closing of the company Audiradio. The publishing industry is suffering, with a structural crisis exacerbated by the economic and financial situation of the country. Online advertising, however, is in excellent health. In Italy, the Internet is the second largest advertising medium after television. Cinema, after a period of decline in 2010, has seen an increase in sales and advertising

[5] A portal represents a general access to tourism facilities as is the case with Expedia.com while a website is specific to the hotel that is booked. In other words the portal brings the customer to choose a particular website in order to reserve the room or service desired.

revenues. Below-the-line advertising has recently picked up. Promotions are the preferred form of communication by businesses (over 30 % of the activities of marketing). Direct marketing, which in 2011 represented 18 % of the investments, in the previous year saw a decline of 5 %, most likely owing to the growing interest in more innovative promotion activities. Investments in web marketing, in fact, increased by 47 %.

In 2014, companies invested about 4 billion in online communications between above-the-line (online advertising 55 %) and below-the-line (web marketing 45 %). Companies that invest in the Web comprise 25 %, a proportion higher than those which invest in television (4 %) and radio (5.5 %). There are different types of online advertising: display, video advertising, search, classified directories, mobile and so on. The search type of advertising has the most demand (48 %), followed by display advertising (32 %), classified directory advertising (included under "other") and social networks (20 %). Video advertising is only used by 12 % of online advertisers, and mobile by 15 %.

1.4 Conclusions

Based on the discussion in the following seven chapters of this volume and the Appendix it is clear that the debate in Italy is not much different from that which has transpired in other EU countries and in countries with large markets and a sales tax system based on states and a federal income tax that requires corporations to turn over to the government a significant percentage of their overall profits. Thus, the dilemma of taxing significant cross-border transactions, and impeding the systematic use of low- or no-tax jurisdictions, has the potential of eroding the national tax bases which makes it difficult to continue with the current status quo. The status quo requires a robust response on the part of the G20 as a collective body and by individual governments in implementing the recommendations that have come out of the OECD and EU studies and the deliberations of the expert groups assigned the task of making recommendations on the matter. It is clear that immediate action needs to be taken and the direction of that action is discussed in detail in the chapters that follow.

2

The Damages of Fiscal Competition in Europe and Alternatives to Anarchy

Salvatore Biasco

2.1 Introduction

Let us start with a summary.[1] It is not generally understood that in the area of taxation important parts of the regulation of world capitalism are at stake. And the fact has escaped many that—still in the field of taxation—the only truly global rule for any length of time was introduced and signed by a host of countries in October 2014, and concerned the automatic exchange of information among fiscal authorities. While this represents a revolutionary development—given that

[1] This chapter is based on a lecture given at the European Interparliamentary Conference Under Article 13 of the Fiscal Compact (29–30 September 2014), organized during the European Semester of Italian Presidency by the Italian Chamber of Deputies, Palazzo Montecitorio, in the section titled "The coordination of fiscal policies in Europe." Compared to that text, this chapter was extensively remodeled, to make it less technical and more accessible to the non-specialist reader. The author is Professor of International Monetary Economics and was President of the Bicameral Commission for Tax Reform in the XIII Legislature (1996–2001) and author of the White Paper on Corporate Taxation (2007), drawn up by the Commission that bears his name.

S. Biasco (✉)
University of Rome, La Sapienza, Rome, Italy

F. Boccia, R. Leonardi (eds.), *The Challenge of the Digital Economy*,
DOI 10.1007/978-3-319-43690-6_2

it presents some serious problems to holders of a great amount of wealth, to tax evaders and to money launderers—it is nevertheless incomplete. It does not present, in fact, any particular problem for multinationals to *legally* avoid paying taxes, and to subtract them from the country where the income is generated, basically keeping them for themselves. This not only causes a loss of revenue but also distorts competition in their favour. We must tackle a situation whereby companies such as Amazon, Apple and Starbucks and many others are taxed at approximately 2 % on their profits while other producers are subjected to full taxation and labour is overtaxed. Enormous losses of revenue (from tax avoidance, evasion and illegal activities) are at stake, to the tune of as much as 1000 billion euros annually, according to the previous Commission's own estimates.[2]

The argument goes that the nation-state is becoming less effective thanks to the extent of financial globalization. But in this field this is true only in part. The nation-states (especially the European ones) have not lost the power of taxation due to globalization but because of tax competition. In fiscal matters, the distortion of European construction is the weak link. And it is from Europe—another Europe—that a turnaround could be initiated if the Union were to act as a catalyst for countries to impose—by strength of their number and the voice of reason (and with the same political will that led to the agreement on information-sharing)—a worldwide standard in the taxation of multinational corporation. The frontier to be crossed is represented by a system of unitary taxation of multinational corporation—that is, a taxation not fragmented, unlike that which exists now under the international conventions. This would require the creation of a consolidated taxation system on a global basis, apportioned according to an index of actual activity in the individual countries. In Europe, such a transition could be an opportunity to combine the achievement of tax harmonization in the field of direct taxation with an enlargement of the EU budget, as well as with procedures to compensate those weaker countries that will lose the benefits they have reaped previously from tax competition. Let us now explore these issues more thoroughly.

---

[2] Recently, Algirdas Semeta, Commissioner for Taxation and Customs Union, also referred to the same number. As a reminder, the Union's budget is approximately 150 billion euros.

2.2 What Is Missing Is a European Model

While it goes without saying that the European level is the appropriate one to pursue a programme for a U-turn in macroeconomic management, institutional architecture and, of course, financial regulation, it is not equally obvious that the same is true in the field of direct taxation. The latter currently resides in a political sphere whereby taxation is the autonomous responsibility of individual countries—as if internal tax systems were not shaped in various ways by continental (and global) interactions.

In the field of direct taxation, Europe today is pervaded by a tax competition that has found, and finds, legitimacy in a neoliberal vision of how the Union should operate. This vision has ruled out any idea that the Union could take upon itself the management of fiscal matters, and has placed competition among States as paramount, notwithstanding the fact that this has led to significant losses in fiscal revenue from the income generated by the more mobile factors which consequently had to be compensated by the taxation of those less mobile factors—labour and property. The point is not simply to remove regimes that are particularistic and "harmful"—in relation to state aid aimed at foreign investors only (a goal pursued in an incomplete way, however)—but to create a uniform and coherent tax structure for Europe. In this period of a weak European commitment by leaders, and of a decidedly weakening momentum in public opinion (to say the least), such a proposal may seem radical, but it is an issue that must be put on the table. The ultimate aim should be to recover revenue lost through tax competition, compensating the weaker countries that had benefited from intra-Union competition, as well as starting a concrete process of substantially reducing the taxation of labour (which would otherwise remain a mere admonishment in official documents). Finally, it should also lead to the identification of sources of revenue that could significantly increase the Community's budget. And it is no small matter in this context if Europe were to place itself in the vanguard of the proposal to overcome what, today, are the outdated assumptions that govern international agreements on transnational taxation, and to define a global standard for taxation that responds to the new realities of integrated capitalism.

Not only is there currently no European model for direct taxation, but there are not even mutually conforming codes on taxation and regulation. In the area of direct taxation the convergence towards common solutions for national systems takes place only through the imitation of schemes introduced in other European countries that individual countries choose in a discretionary bricolage. The variety of solutions makes it difficult to refer to any single benchmark system.

Even in terms of principles, there is no uniformity if we consider that the principle of progressivity in personal taxation is disregarded by many countries, especially in Eastern Europe where a *flat tax* is adopted (only slightly adjusted by allowing differentiated deductions). This suggests that the European social model is becoming an abstraction which applies to a limited number of member states.

2.3 Convergence Is Not Always Positive

We must not assume, however, that convergence in tax systems is always a good thing and can ensure a more efficient functioning of the internal market, nor that it leads to a more equitable taxation system. It is not positive when convergence is not an organized design with specific objectives or an overall rationale, but simply the outcome of a fiscal chase made for fear of losing taxable bases. It cannot even be said that the generalization of any particular scheme leads in the end to a race to the bottom in its specific field of impact (whatever this concerns: regulation, fiscal treatment of the holdings, tax rates, e-commerce, tax bases, controls, and so on) because that race is always resumed with an added or new element.[3]

[3] A good example of this is the taxation of holding companies. The system that benefited them for the fiscal treatment of profits and capital gain, called Participation Exemption (Pex), was gradually extended from the Benelux countries to almost all other European countries at the beginning of 2000, to prevent the relocation of their holding companies. It would have been necessary for a European initiative to have been undertaken to prevent such a change and for the pre-existing tax system (of tax credit on dividends) to have been made systemic and truly European. But that never happened, and countries were left to decide what to do on their own. However, the spread of the Pex system has not put an end to tax competition because the latter has been transferred to the domain of regulatory provisions in the legislation of some countries (for example, the UK and the

There are many examples of this pattern that have been endorsed by the European Court of Justice in the name of a mistaken fundamentalism with which it interprets the "freedom of establishment" (beginning with the unhappy sentence for the Cadbury Schweppes case).[4] The Court has never been particularly attentive to the systemic consequences of its decisions, but is highly sensitive to the liberal bent of European integration.

2.4 We Need a "Grand Design": Can We Find It in Recent Developments?

What we need is a large-scale plan for the convergence of and harmonization in fiscal matters and not occasional developments, competition or judgments by the Court. Even those who think that the Court has performed its institutional task in compliance with the Treaties (with excessive zeal, in the author's opinion) agree that the Court is not, nor can it be, the appropriate instrument for the resolution of the contradictions that dominate the present state of affairs. Furthermore, the Court

---

Netherlands). These countries facilitate opportunistic behaviour by enabling companies established in them to effectively have their management and tax residence in a another country and, at the same time, by allowing them to lock down the ownership by adopting a sheme of increased voting rights for stable shareholders (see, for example, the case of the transfer of the Fiat headquarters to the Netherlands and the fiscal office to the UK). As a result, a greater recognition of increased voting rights of the major shareholder has spread to other European fiscal systems. It is inevitable that, in the same way, the regime of "patent box" will become more diffuse as part of the ongoing competition to attract corporations to relocate their headquarters. It allows for the imposition of an ad hoc tax (between 5 and 10 %) on profits related to the use of patents. It is also called the "innovation box" because of its apparent purpose of encouraging innovation and skilled jobs in Research and Development, while in reality it rewards the commercialization of existing patents rather than the development of new ones. Given that with competion there is no end, there are countries (such as the UK) where 100 % of the profits earned on products that fall into this regime are recognized as valid even when the holding of the patents is secondary to their production.

[4] The Cadbury Schweppes sentence was issued in connection with an appeal by the parent company settled in Britain against the national tax authorities. The case concerned the profits of two subsidiaries established in Ireland in order to qualify for the host's lower rate of profits taxation. The lawsuit was filed (in 2000) against the British tax authorities which, according to the law in force in that country, obliged the parent company to compensate for the difference between taxes paid abroad and taxes that should have been paid in the UK if the company had been resident in that country. The Court (in September 2006) ruled in favour of Cadbury on the principle enshrined in the Treaties of the "freedom of establishment", which from then on has become the principle that deprived individual national authorities of the power to limit tax competition.

certainly cannot replace the necessary political debate between the social forces and the nation states whose role it is to make the essential decisions within the appropriate institution.

We need to ask ourselves the question of whether the three major advances in recent years in articulating a course of action to confront the problems of fiscal governance at the international level relate to a far-reaching vision of the future workings of the Union and are "grand designs". These advances include the elimination of "harmful" competition, the countering of the use of tax havens and the intended launch of the Common Consolidated Tax Base (CCTB), the basic design of a common consolidated base for the taxation of corporations.

2.4.1 "Harmful" and "Non-harmful" Tax Competition

It is only since the mid-1990s that it has become clear that the actions set out by the OECD to address the issue of tax havens would not have been credible if the EU member states had not been seriously committed to removing the "particularistic" and preferential regimes for foreign capital provided in their territories that benefit large companies and non-resident wealthy individuals.[5] Those tax regimes have been identified as constituting "harmful" competition, which thus has been distinguished in a subjective manner from "non-harmful" competition. How do we define the latter? "Fair", "virtuous" or "beneficial" in nature?

It is all well and good that those regimes are being removed. But this does not mean that there are not still niches outside of the law and murky areas in which companies can benefit from operating in one country over another as, for example, in the field of patents and licences. Formal discriminatory allowances do not exhaust the picture. There persists favourable treatment of those corporations who relocate and benefit from weaker controls than in their countries of origin. Even the definition of taxable income plays a role in attracting foreign capital. And the actions of the Court have affirmed the dubious notion

[5] "Particularistic" was the definition used owing to the fact that it was not possible for residents to access the same regime.

that any tax initiative by the nation-state is acceptable if it does not discriminate between foreign and domestic operators.

It should have attracted attention that, within the limits of the success of the ban on "harmful competition," policies directed towards a general reduction in tax rates and to the narrowing of the tax base tended (and tend) to be the dominant mode of tax competition, especially in the case of the new member countries spurred by the example of Ireland.[6] The abatement of tax rates on profits will certainly be non-discriminatory, but, as most of the economic literature tells us, it can also distort the allocation of capital and production, resulting in a negative spillover effect on those countries that are affected. We should perhaps be asking ourselves if there is such a thing as virtuous, fair or beneficial tax competition. The arguments in favour of competition are well known, but they are overwhelmed by the evidence that "beneficial" competition tends to distort the structure of personal taxation,[7] or brings about a loss in overall taxable income which is thus offset by taxes on non-mobile factors or by a reduction in public spending. It also provides incentives for profit-shifting, resulting in an inefficient level of public goods, and it tends to lead to business decisions that distort the single market as it brings capital to where it is taxed less and not necessarily where it is used most productively.

Therefore, it would not constitute a "grand design" to remove the unfair competition even if it does represent a significant advancement. It would represent a grand design if[8]:

1. the harmonization of the rate of corporate tax was still listed as a legitimate medium-term objective of the EU. As an intermediate step, it would be appropriate to keep differences in corporate tax within a predetermined range (but with a common tax base). Although the

---

[6] Ireland rate on profits is fixed at 12.5 %. The average tax rate on profits in Europe has being decreasing from 45 % in 1980 to 24 % in 2014, with an ever narrowing variance. The trend is contininuing.

[7] It impinges upon progressivity in personal taxation, because a high marginal rate on personal income tax make convenient for rich people to transform personal incomes into capital incomes.

[8] A graphic notation: the bullet points indicate lines of action and possible contents that are desirable for the Union to pursue.

advantages of agglomeration can allow larger countries to maintain competitive with a higher than average rate, this is true to a certain extent only and in any case does not justify the lack of a minimum tax rate on corporations (at least 25 %) in order to curb the continuous exodus of companies from one country to another in the pursuit of more favourable taxation, an exodus which is often obtained with real promotion campaigns (that are not considered to be "unfair").
2. the EU moved towards the establishment of uniform controls aimed at keeping in check the gains and losses in taxation that generate the difference between taxation on labour and taxation on production.

The weaker countries would be helped to compete on the basis of real economic factors and not by offering facilities designed to infringe the laws of others; for this, and other reasons, a more consistent European budget is needed.

2.4.2 Countering the Tax Havens

Are the actions taken by the EU to counter tax havens in the wake of the OECD model of cooperation part of a grand design? Undoubtedly, the fact that we have arrived at outlining three focus areas to address the problem represents a clear step forward. These areas are (1) the lack of transparency and exchange of information, namely the "service of secrecy" that is offered by tax havens, (2) the lack of substantial activity associated with the location of a company in a tax haven, (3) the low or zero taxation of foreign corporations (vis-à-vis that of local residents).

So far, rule enforcement has focused almost exclusively on the first problem, on the basis of the OECD project that is being implemented at the European level. Despite this limitation, we should rejoice at the system moving from an approach where financial information is provided on a targeted request basis to a model where information is obtained automatically with direct access to the financial data of another country (as of September 2017). Certainly, information provided through the previous international regime did not prove to be particularly effective in curbing the harmful competitive advantage that tax havens provide if we consider that the amount of funds held offshore has increased dramatically during the past decade. The fact that, on 30 October 2014, in Berlin, 58 countries signed the agreement for the automatic exchange of information held in their financial system is highly significant. As already stated, it is perhaps the only global rule that has been adopted by a large group of countries for decades—a rule that promises to create a new world order in taxation if it is applied in all financial centres. What sufficed was the sheer determination of the USA and other major countries to arrive at this outcome for reasons of security (after 9/11) and to stop tax evasion. This has made it impossible for a country that wants to be respected in the international community to avoid joining the agreement with others. Even Luxembourg and other European countries that were considered to be tax havens—as well as the Cayman Islands, Singapore, San Marino and others—have agreed to comply. The pressure to join is clear, as even Liechtenstein and Monte Carlo have signed the agreement, while other countries have announced that they will do the same. It is a leap forward in countering illegal capital movements and tax evasion.[9]

As good as this is, it is necessary to maintain a vigilant attitude in order for the commitments made by the countries to actually be put in place and for these countries to express a real ability and will to oblige local operators to collect and systematically transmit data to be exchanged according to the agreed standard of protocols and models referred to as the *Common Report and Due Diligence Standard*. Further, there must be a system of effective sanctions for those countries that do not comply. The banking licence for those financial institutions that do not cooperate, boycott or prove particularly active in promoting tax avoidance should be withdrawn. Moreover, the difficulty and delays in applying the new standard in all of the financial centres must not be seen as an opportunity for some subscriber (within or outside of the EU) to delay in implementing the system.

[9] At the time of writing there are more than 70 signatory countries. To appreciate this milestone let us remember that it took 11 years from when the European directive on savings of 2003 was launched to close loopholes and extend the scope of application to a sufficient range of financial instruments. That directive aimed at making financial income generated elsewhere subject to taxation in the country of residence (with the exception of Luxembourg, Austria and Ireland) but its correction was long retarded owing to the presence in Europe of countries that took advantage of such loopholes.

It should not be difficult (by simplifying technical requirements) to obtain an international *taxpayer identification number*—first at the European level and then at the global level. In the field of security it was sufficient that the political will was such that it allowed the creation at a global level of a system which provides access to Interpol records from across the world simply through a passport identification number; the same should and could be done in the field of taxation if there was the same political will. It is important for the EU and the OECD to standardize the rules, but it would be even better if the process were led by a UN agency. Notwithstanding the fact that Europe entrusts the study of the issue to the OECD, this institution does not have the legitimacy or territorial representation to make it global. It is not an intergovernmental organization, but a research centre for a number of advanced countries (including those inclined to act as dubious financial magnets).

2.4.3 The Ineffectiveness of Countering the Use of Tax Havens for Fictitious Activities

In terms of transparency and the exchange of information, the system is certainly changing in the right direction with enhanced coordination and integration aimed at weakening the role of tax havens in financial flows. However, in terms of tax avoidance through fictitious activities located in low-tax areas, the counteracting steps still lie with individual countries. Practices associated with tax avoidance will not disappear even with a fully automatic system for the exchange of information. At the heart of the problem are the artificial constructs creating activities of convenience in the tax havens and using them for advantageous triangulations. To counter such imaginative schemes, countries apply a set of defensive actions under the guidelines of the so-called Controlled Foreign Companies (CFC) approach.

The reclassification of budgets by fiscal administrations under this approach remains, however, an inefficient and cumbersome process, aimed at attributing to the national company all or part of the profits generated by the foreign subsidiary located in low-tax countries. The European context reveals the heterogeneity of each of the essential characteristics that condition the application of CFC rules—from restrictions on the deduction of taxes paid elsewhere; the failure to recognize specific costs; the introduction of withholding taxes on payments made to blacklisted countries; the presumptions of internal residence of the company settled abroad; rules on transfer prices; a restrictive interpretation of notions of control and connection between firms; to the monitoring of derivatives and financial mechanisms that contribute to *profit-shifting*; and so on.[10] In whatever way it is applied, the CFC approach is not systematic; it implies subjective judgments and, moreover, creates administrative problems, uncertainties and difficulties in the compliance with or in the provision of contrasting evidence. In this way it contributes to a non-monetary fiscal competition by making attractive, in a kind of vicious circle, those (advanced) countries that allow companies the undisturbed use of tax loopholes. Not surprisingly, decisions of the European Court of Justice have diminished the effectiveness of protective measures adopted by individual countries affected by this competition by imposing a disapplication of such measures (or their mitigation) for fear that applying them within the EU will impact on the freedom of establishment within the single market.

2.5 Google, Apple and so on ...

Defensive actions are pointless when the profits generated in Europe by multinational corporations located in the continent are *legally* transferred—emptied—to branches in locations with low or zero taxation. This can happen as a result of the European countries that acknowledge, allow or agree with multinationals' use of such practices. These countries focus on the externalities generated by the establishment of multinational operational headquarters in their territories (in terms of well-paid and skilled jobs, the use, in situ, of financial services and other economic benefits), rather than on the potential tax revenues, which are allowed to vanish. Recently, attention has focused on cases of multinational

[10] However we must note that since 2012 the UK has abandoned the presumption of tax avoidance for the activity of an enterprise located in a tax haven.

companies such as Apple, Amazon, Starbucks, HP and Google.[11] These companies represent only the tip of the iceberg in a widespread phenomenon. As a result, the EU has opened an investigation in which Luxembourg is failing to adequately cooperate by refusing to reveal details of its tax system.

The mechanism of *tax avoidance* is fairly uniform. Multinationals use the prices of internal transactions to attribute a low profit margin to activities in countries with high taxation and where they have a significant share of the market. Theoretically, they direct profits to the country where their parent unit is established, but from this base they make deductible payments to subsidiaries that have been created on an ad hoc basis outside of the EU, in tax havens (with low or zero taxation), for the purpose of "providing" loans, or the use of the trademark, patents or other services. Sometimes these subsidiaries simply have a legal right (*economic ownership*) to a sort of usufruct on income of the parent company (which maintains the *legal ownership*). Needless to say, the headquarters are located in countries such as Luxembourg, the Netherlands, Ireland and, in part, Belgium, where the taxation is low at the outset (sometimes agreed in advance),[12] and where there is no withholding tax on payments for non-material services abroad[13] and the practice of (fictitiously) dislocating branches is not called into question. Neither is it compulsory in some of these countries to give evidence of a subsidiary's budget if the operating unit (that is, where strategic decisions are made) is located abroad and the subsidiary is 100 % owned and unincorporated. It would be interesting to follow the many imaginative cases of corporate fiscal practices. To cite just a few concrete examples, it may happen that the profits before tax declared by the European parent company of Starbucks, located in the Netherlands, have generated only 342,000 euros in taxes in

[11] But also Ikea, PepsiCo, FedEx, Procter & Gamble, Vodafone, Microsoft, and many more.

[12] Agreements are made through the so-called tax ruling or advance pricing agreement (APA), a transaction tax agreement, where companies ask in advance what their taxation will be upon their relocation. "Normal" taxation rates are then applied (which do not result in "harmful competition"—for example, 25 % in the Netherlands), but the abatement of the tax base or other provisions reduce dramatically the taxable profits.

[13] Such a tax exists in Italy, for example, although it is only 5 % for countries that have subscribed to a convention and is 30 % for the others. In each of the tax havens within the Union there are no withholding taxes on payments for intangibles.

2013 (for which a loss was reported, as was the case in 2012 and 2011) on European sales of 92.5 million euros (over 55 % of which goes to cover costs for rights to the trademark "paid" to subsidiaries based in tax havens).[14] Amazon, located in Luxembourg, adopts the same practices, but in this case the payments for intangible services are paid to a subsidiary in Luxembourg, which is virtually free of taxes (taxable profits are 3 cents per 1000 euros of turnover).[15] Incidentally, it is estimated that Luxembourg is the home of 40,000 holding companies. Google uses a triangulation of Ireland, the Netherlands and Bermuda (2 cents of taxable income per 1000 euro of turnover). Even more striking is the case of Apple—not so much because out of almost 20 billion profits it pays more or less 8 million (less than 1 %) euros in global taxes (the average of the three budgets for the period 2011–13), but because it channelled the actual profits in deductible payments to three subsidiaries of its Irish head office that do not have a physical residence declared anywhere in the world, one of which has never published its financial statements (which is legal according to Irish law).[16]

By observing the situation from the point of view of the firms that compete with the ones mentioned (or similar cases), we can see to what extent tax avoidance distorts competition in the market (as well as being detrimental to the finances of those countries which are deprived of the tax revenue of their competence), in that it gives companies that are

[14] A British survey highlights that since its arrival in Britain in 1988, Starbucks paid until 2012 cumulatively taxes for 11.5 million euros against sales of 4.5 billion euros.

[15] Ordering a book worth 50 euro, for instance, generates an integrated taxable profit of 1.5 cents. Amazon has eight mega warehouses in Great Britain and 6000 employees; It has a large number of employees in France, and Germany, but the bulk of the profits go to its Luxembourg headquarter where it has 200 employees.

[16] This was raised in the US Senate's inquiry into Apple. Explaining which legal loopholes make it possible implies to going into technical details. In a nutshell, companies in Ireland are considered foreign companies if their effective management is abroad. At the same time, they are also considered foreign companies for the fiscal administration of the US if they are legally established outside national borders. Moreover, in Ireland they are not obliged to publish their financial statement if they are unincorporated (as Apple's subsidiaries are). In major European markets, Apple fixes (from Ireland) wholesale prices to subsidiaries in order to limit the profits taxed locally. In 2011, for example, Apple declared local losses of the local holding company in Germany and France and paid taxes for 10.5 million euros in the UK on sales worth more than 1.3 billion euros.

virtually tax-free the possibility of cannibalizing competitors unless the latter are able to imitate them and follow them in this dangerous game.[17]

2.6 … And the Digital Economy: Two Possible Solutions

Similar constructs can exist in the entire digital economy,[18] when companies that sell services on line can have access to the Internet from any location. Sometimes these services do not result in the delivery of a physical object (for example, music, software and so on). It is even difficult to pinpoint exactly where profits are diverted, because it is difficult to identify where the server—considered to be the company headquarters—is located. It may be on some platform outside of territorial waters. But even in standard cases, companies in the digital economy may not require a stable organization in the country where they sell and are therefore not subject to taxation on site. Among other things, the power of tax authorities to *enforce* payments where the sales take place vanishes as is evident with the application of VAT.

There are two possible solutions to make activities and incomes subject to taxation that would otherwise be avoided: one is based on a greater reach and one which can be more easily implemented; the other is an organic and potentially global solution, but it would require the same kind of *political determination* that led to the agreement on information being provided automatically.

[17]This paper was already written (the report to the European Parliaments is dated 30 September 2014) when, a month later, the Junker case broke (Prime Minister of Luxemburg for 15 years) on the secret agreements signed by his country with many multinational companies to obtain settlement in exchange for the remission of taxes. So far, only agreements brokered by the consulting firm Pricewaterhouse Coopers have emerged. If I was fully aware of the existence of such practices how was it possible that they were not known to other political leaders in Europe? Perhaps they have not stopped this practice because tax competition is beneficial? Moreover, how could it have escaped the European Parliament's notice that Junker had been for decades Luxembourg Prime Minister?

[18]The digital economy represents 5 % of GDP in Western countries and is rapidly growing. It is plausible to assume it will reach double-digit levels soon.

2.7 The Digital Tax and the Belated Reactions of Governments

Within the first approach, the way out is to switch to a principle of taxation at source, at least for the trading online of intangibles, by applying a flat withholding tax on the value of sales and assuming that income has been generated where there are logistics centres, where the company has significant market share or where substantial economic activity takes place and the value is created. In fact (even if not in law), it would be nothing more than a duplicate of VAT (that, considered on this account as a direct tax, must not be allowed to fall on the consumer). This is a way of buffering the possibility that transfer prices or the absence of a stable organization evaporates the tax base in the country where the income is produced (and sometimes even where the company has its place of residence). At the opposite end, the risks of double taxation should not be ignored.

In essence, we are talking about a rethink of the international system of world distribution of taxable income based on bilateral treaties to prevent double taxation. Termed the principle of *Home State Taxation*, it is a principle that taxes revenue at the source, and recognizes the amount already paid in taxes elsewhere while going through the pyramid chain of ownership towards the country where the headquarters of the company resides.[19] This principle assumes a physical presence and a stable organization in each foreign territory. This solution worked well when the digital economy did not exist, as there was little opportunity to shift profits via internal transfer pricing, and little ability to route service activities

[19] The first tranche of taxation goes to the state where the company operates with a stable organization (in practice, the local head company in the area). The state in which the parent company operates upstream applies the second tranche according to its own criteria, and so on, recognizing what has already been paid in income taxes in those countries with which it has signed a treaty against double taxation. Today, the principle of *Home State Taxation* is undermined not only by the management of transfer pricing in internal trade of conglomerates, but also by the fact that in the digital economy a stable organization in the country of sales is not necessary. However, the new EU rules on *indirect* taxes, VAT, (which came into force in 2015) states that companies that sell, online, certain services (and with a sales turnover exceeding certain thresholds) should identify themselves in every EU consumer country.

through tax havens or to do without a permanent organization, but these days this is obsolete.

Taxing at source on the basis of sales (and not income) is a defensive solution with many risks, but it is linear and able to provide some cover to a situation that is quickly getting out of hand. However, it is not easy to erect a barrier between the digital economy and a non-digital one, and above all, to do it purely for tax reasons. Moreover, it does not solve cases such as Starbucks and Pepsi Cola, which do not sell anything online.

It should not be said that governments are not now taking remedial measures after being late in realizing what has been happening. The EU (and the OECD) has long instituted study committees for the launching of a digital tax along the lines referred to above as a buffer solution. However, a European directive for giving rise to a single market in this field is all but imminent, and thus, having waited for this for years, many European countries have announced possible interventions but abstain from approving their own solutions.[20]

In any case these countries have come to realize that they have been deprived of a great deal of tax revenue which has been diverted abroad through the practices of multinational enterprises. They have therefore taken steps to retrieve these receipts. Whenever there are sufficient elements (managers, employee, offices operating in the country and email communications) they act on the presumption (to be proven) that the multinational enterprises in question have operated in the country with a shadow stable organization. In other words, they maintain that operations were conducted not from abroad but by intermediary organizations operating in the country and unknown to the fiscal authorities whose profits generated on site would have been subject to ordinary taxation if this organization had been registered. In the cases in which such revenue is actually retrieved this is a result of complex negotiations with companies, which always claim to have acted in line with the rules. Today multinationals understand that the damage to their reputation that comes from such contention is worse than losing some profits, and thus they are

[20] The solution put forward for Italy provides a withholding tax of 25 % for online sales, unless the seller establishes a stable organization in the country, in which case it would be taxed on an ordinary basis.

forced to come to a compromise (that closes invariably far from the expectations of the governments concerned). Currently, Italy and the UK are leading the way.[21] However, it is a state of play in which each country acts individually and which, for now, is limited to emblematic cases. This does not mean that such actions do not have discouraging effects.

Even the EU has taken notice after the outcry in the press on the issue of tax avoidance. Its strategy is to verify whether the preliminary agreements that a few countries have undertaken with multinationals (agreement, however, that other countries are gradually introducing in their tax ruling, as in the case of Italy, for example) presuppose preferential taxation, and hence state aids. The road is a long and contested one and for now has produced only small change in obliging some firms to return irrelevant sums of money to those countries responsible for allowing tax avoidance (Luxembourg and the Netherlands in this case), with the paradoxical result that the fiscal incentives have already attracted companies while the host country has used that same revenue to attract other firms.[22]

In addition, deterrence through transparency is a line that has recently been followed. This line provides for automatic information on tax rulings that companies enjoy in the European context, as well as on their profits and turnover in any single country in order to put member countries in the condition to verify the coherence of firms' fiscal statements.[23]

[21] Italy has agreed with Apple a payment of 318 mln euros out of an initial request of 979 mln for profits generated in the country in the years 2008–14. As part of the agreement, Apple will establish a stable organization. The weapon that was wielded to convince the company to end litigation was the threat of a criminal investigation. At present, other cases are open with Google, Amazon, Twitter and a few other giants. In the UK, the case against Google has been closed with the payment of a modest sum of 130 million pounds for the period 2005–15. The UK has approved a levy of 25 % on sales as a tax on (imputed) profits obtained by multinationals within the national boundaries (and applicable to those operating without stable organizations and through offshore branches). It is called the Diverted Profit Tax. See Chap. 7 for more details.

[22] At the moment only the investigations of Fiat (Luxembour) and Starbucks(Netherland) have been completed and the host countries forced to "retrieve" almost 30 mln euros in each case. The last case that has been opened involves MacDonald. As we go to press Margrethe Vestager, the EU's competition commissioner, announced on 3 September 2016 that Apple must return 13 billion euros to the Irish government for taxes on profits due for the period 1991–2007. These taxes were avoided thanks to the preferential treatment offered by the Irish government but considered by the EU as a state aid. Both Apple and the Irish government have appealed.

[23] It has to be singled out that, within the BEPS project, Europe has expressed an intention to limit the fiscal recognition for interest paid by a foreign branch to its parent company. This would check

From any perspective, all this entails chaotic and complicated solutions which, at best, may work as a weak obstacle and lead to some restraint in the use of questionable practices and rules (as we can already see from the changes introduced in the Irish legislation).[24] However, these are neither systematic nor collective solutions, while a solution with these features could exist and could become the international standard on corporate taxation.

2.8 The Organic and Wide-Ranging Solution

The "grand design" in this field, would ideally be one which jointly resolves all the problems we have discussed; it would be a design that aims to move towards a *unitary taxation of transnational corporations*. Unitary taxation means taxation on a company's integrated global income. This principle allows for the achievement of an effective and organic overcoming of the previous international taxation standard whose contents were designed 100 years ago when today's reality of multinational corporations did not exist and nor was there the free movement of capital. Such corporations are not made up of a series of local units to be taxed separately at different sites in the same way as if they were independent units, as the current convention against double taxation tends to see them. Instead, they form, together, a strictly connected business unit that derives its competitive capabilities by combining economic activities in individual locations as well as by exploiting the technology and knowledge belonging to that unit. If they are a single body of which each branch is an organic part then as a single

the convenience for ad hoc budget adjustments aimed at shifting taxable income from a high-tax country towards a low-tax one. Yet the intention of introducing a kind of exit tax for productive activities or assets transferred abroad for fiscal reasons belongs to the same objective of curbing special practices. It might be asked whether this chasing of each of the devices that firms use for fiscal planning is better than having a fiscal harmonization of tax rates on profits. See the following chapter by Russo on the BEPS project.

[24] Under international pressure, Ireland has proposed to approve a legislation that would set the profit tax rate charged under its patent box scheme at 6.25 % (half of the ordinary rate of 12.5 %), and which would be applicable only to intellectual products coming from research carried out in the country. So far a great deal of research has been carried out abroad, as in the case of Google.

body they must be treated. Hence reference for taxing them should be to their *worldwide, consolidated* budget. Multinationals should submit their profit declarations in every country where they operate, and then their integrated profits should be taxed in a unitary way, according to an agreed formula for the apportioning of income which would reflect their actual presence in each country. The formula must take into account the distribution of (1) physical units (or costs) of the workforce employed, (2) physical assets used (excluding intangible assets) and (3) sales realized in each country. The economic literature has discussed this point. Finding agreed unitary accounting criteria to compile financial statements is a relatively simple solution given the current existence of accepted accounting standards.

A scheme of this kind, which eliminates internal transactions, would eradicate the economic convenience of making fictitious constructs in tax havens or moving profits around the globe through internal trade pricing. When the conglomerate is taken as a unitary centre, the final result makes the location of subsidiaries or the transfer prices irrelevant. Companies themselves would benefit from the scheme, since it allows them to offset profits and losses obtained in different countries and to reduce the cost of compliance. Fiscal authorities would also benefit, as they would not have to reformulate company accounts and implement complex defensive measures along the lines of the CFC's approach, from which many disputes have arisen which often involve other administrations and require complicated and never-ending mediations. This new system needs to be brought about in the name of a just and ethical tax system, as well as the regulation of world capitalism that is in line with today's reality.

The unitary taxation regime also has the advantage of being able to be applied by a group of countries even before an international agreement makes it the new standard in taxation. But it would still be appropriate to extend it to a global level. Europe should lead the way in applying the regime globally by taking advantage of the support that it enjoys in Canada and the USA, where it is included in the provisions of the Dodd-Frank Act, and where many states are already adopting it to protect themselves from tax competition from other states.

2.9 The European Common Consolidated Tax Base (CCTB)

Can we conclude that the Common Consolidated Tax Base passed by the European Parliament in 2012 and then in 2016 is a "grand design"? It could be, but it stops at the doorway. In its current form, it is significantly limited in scope.

1. The CCTB should be mandatory, whereas the current project makes it optional, meaning that two parallel systems would co-exist and companies could choose between them, forcing the national authorities to deal with both systems. It would end up being the 29th EU tax system, not a distinct and truly European system of company taxation (a system that, at best, the EU itself could administer retaining a portion of its proceeds for its budget).
2. It should provide a harmonization of taxes on profits, because otherwise it would still keep alive a tax competition aimed at capturing the location of firms and continues a race to reduce the taxation of multinational firms. In place of such an outcome, it is preferable that the harmonization of tax rates be combined with an additional criterion among those proposed to apportion the consolidated profits of multinationals (so far, labour, physical assets and sales), a criterion whose rationale is to benefit the countries with lower incomes and compensate them for the loss of competition through an appropriate policy instrument (it could consist in an inversely proportional weight assigned to some measure based on the per capita income of the member states).
3. Finally, it should refer to the consolidated global profits, whereas at the moment it requires the consolidation of only the profits coming from European operations. Thus, the European tax base remains separate from the non-European one, thereby leaving firms the opportunity to exclude intermediary companies located in tax havens. Profit-shifting and ficticious activities continue to be a problem and attempts to put an end to these avoidance measures have proved so far to be completely insufficient.

2.10 What Are the Prospects?

Even in a watered-down version, the CCTB project risks never being launched or being scaled down to a project without the "*consolidated*" factor (where all that is achieved is a harmonization of the tax base). Ireland, the Netherlands and the UK, to varying degrees, have detached themselves from the project. Moreover, if it is to be launched the project needs to resolve some significant technical details. It also needs the unanimous vote of the European Council which must not be taken for granted.

This raises another sore point for European integration, one that requires unanimity of the 28 member states for decisions to be binding in tax matters, plus the assent of the Council of Ministers, the Commission and the European Parliament—and all with the supposed collaboration of those European countries that have acted as tax havens and continue to attract capital through questionable means.

Unless we overcome the provision of unanimity in fiscal decisions, it will always be difficult to achieve concrete results on these issues, let alone implement policies that are organic and truly European.

Unanimity can also make it difficult to decide what portion of tax receipts raised under the above system—if administered by the Union—should be devoted to a stronger European budget (that may include receipts from a carbon tax and from taxes on financial transactions). A stronger budget is needed to draw resources to compensate those countries that may feel harmed by policies that challenge tax competition. But, of course, it is also designed to achieve other obvious objectives of strengthening the European infrastructure and supporting economic activity.

European countries have not lost fiscal autonomy because of globalization but because of internal competition, as has already been stated. They can regain autonomy only if they act collectively. It takes political impetus to address the issues of the principles involved.

Obviously the project aimed at curbing tax competition is not the only one that the EU needs, but it is also not secondary. If the EU continues to allow countries to embezzle each other's tax bases and legitimizes the deindustrialization of some to the benefit of others, it will embody a serious distortion that—coupled with the prospects of low long-term growth and high unemployment—will limit its capacity to grow and prosper.

3

Base Erosion and Profit Shifting

Raffaele Russo

3.1 What BEPS Is and Why It Is Important to Address It

BEPS is an acronym for "base erosion and profit shifting" and refers to tax planning strategies that exploit gaps and mismatches in tax rules to make profits "disappear" for tax purposes or to shift profits to locations where there is little or no real activity but the taxes are low, resulting in little or no overall corporate tax being paid. Developments brought about by globalization and the digitalization of the economy increasingly put a strain on the existing international tax rules, which are still often grounded in a bricks-and-mortar economic environment rather than the current environment of global players, which is characterized by the increasing importance of intangibles and risk management.

The developments have opened up opportunities to shift profits to locations where little business activity takes place and where these profits

R. Russo (✉)
OECD Centre for Tax Policy and Administration, Paris, France

F. Boccia, R. Leonardi (eds.), *The Challenge of the Digital Economy*,
DOI 10.1007/978-3-319-43690-6_3

are subject to low taxation or no taxation at all. This has given rise to great concern, particularly against the background of the global financial crisis which saw individual income taxes and VAT being raised in most countries. In the area of taxation, historically, the core work of the OECD has been to develop, on the basis of international consensus, common standards to eliminate double taxation for cross-border trade and investments. These standards are embodied in the OECD Model Tax Convention, which currently serves as the basis for over 3000 bilateral tax treaties and the Transfer Pricing Guidelines, which provide common standards for allocating income among members of a group of affiliated companies. Today, the goal remains to eliminate double taxation, but in order to do so effectively, it is necessary to close loopholes in the current systems that may result in double non-taxation.

The debate on BEPS reached the highest political level across the world and governments recognized that a change in this legal framework to match tax policies to the modern economic environment would be achieved more effectively through international cooperation. Indeed, as many BEPS strategies take advantage of the interaction between the tax rules of different countries, unilateral and uncoordinated actions would not fully address the problem. In addition, unilateral and uncoordinated actions responding in isolation could actually result in double—and possibly multiple—taxation for business. This would have a negative impact on investment, growth and employment globally. As a consequence, it was clear that an internationally coordinated approach to facilitate and reinforce domestic actions to protect tax bases and provide comprehensive international solutions was very much needed to respond to BEPS issues.

3.1.1 The Report "Addressing Base Erosion and Profit Shifting"

At the November 2012 meeting in Mexico City, the G20 finance ministers requested a report that provided an analysis of BEPS. The report "Addressing Base Erosion and Profit Shifting" (hereinafter Report) was released on February 2013 to provide an in-depth analysis of BEPS, through the identification of its root causes and the problems involved. It pointed out that, in addition to the loss of corporate tax revenue, BEPS could result in unintended competitive advantages for multinational enterprises (MNEs) over smaller or domestic companies and a distortion of investment decisions (towards investment with lower pre-tax but higher after-tax rates of return). Also, BEPS harms citizens' trust in the integrity of the tax system as a whole, thereby undermining voluntary tax compliance. The Report clarified that BEPS must be addressed by legislative measures, chiefly owing to the fact that most BEPS planning is legal under existing rules. Last but not least, the Report called for the development of a coordinated, holistic and comprehensive plan for action.

At the technical level, the Report identified a number of coordinated strategies associated with BEPS in the context of direct taxation, which were broken down into four elements:

- Minimization of taxation in the market country by avoiding a taxable presence, or in the case of a taxable presence, either by shifting gross profits via trading structures or by reducing net profit by maximizing deductions at the level of the payer.
- Low or no withholding tax at source.
- Low or no taxation at the level of the recipient (which can be achieved via low-tax jurisdictions, preferential regimes or hybrid mismatch arrangements) with entitlement to substantial non-routine profits often built up via intra-group arrangements.
- No current taxation of the low-tax profits at the level of the ultimate parent.

The Report was discussed at the February 2013 Moscow G20 meeting of finance ministers, who expressed strong support for the work done and urged the development of a comprehensive Action Plan to tackle BEPS by the time of their next meeting in July 2013.

3.2 The 15-Action BEPS Project: Inclusive and Transparent

In response to the G20 call, an Action Plan to address BEPS was presented in July 2013, when it was fully endorsed by the G20 finance ministers at their meeting of 19 July. The OECD/G20 BEPS Project was launched in September 2013 to develop the measures envisaged in the Action Plan, following the endorsement of G20 leaders at their meeting of 5–6 September in Russia.

3.2.1 15 Actions Focus on Three Pillars: Coherence, Substance and Transparency

The Action Plan set forth 15 actions to address BEPS in a comprehensive and coordinated manner so as to provide a global roadmap that allows governments to collect the tax revenue they need to serve their citizens. At the same time, it gives businesses the certainty they need to invest and grow. The development of the actions in the Action Plan is based on three core concepts: coherence, substance and transparency.

The *first pillar* includes actions that aim to "close the gaps" between tax sovereignties. Under this pillar, actions are taken to neutralize hybrid mismatches and tax arbitrage, reinforce domestic legislation to protect the tax base of countries against shifting of profits in tax havens (technically called Controlled Foreign Companies (CFC) rules), limit interest deductibility (a major source of base erosion) and counter harmful tax practices more effectively. The *second pillar* includes actions that aim to "strengthen existing international standards," by reviewing tax treaties and transfer pricing rules, which work well in many instances but fail in a number of others. The *third and last pillar* includes actions that aim to "ensure greater transparency" between companies and tax administrations, as well as increased certainty. In this respect, the Action Plan provides for mandatory disclosure of aggressive tax schemes and a form of country- by-country reporting by companies to tax administrations on their worldwide allocation of profits. It also requires more transparency between governments with the need for countries to disclose rulings and other tax benefits to their partners and make dispute resolution mechanisms more effective. It finally provides mechanisms to collect better data so as to be able to measure BEPS and carry out the relevant economic analyses. *Two horizontal actions* complement the Action Plan: the first relates to the tax challenges posed by the digital economy and the second relates to the work to develop a multilateral instrument to quickly amend bilateral tax treaties and hence implement the results of the work on BEPS.

While actions to address BEPS have the aim of restoring both source and residence taxation in a number of cases where cross-border income would otherwise go untaxed or would be taxed at very low rates, these actions are not aimed directly at changing the existing international standards on the allocation of taxing rights on cross-border income. We list in Box 3.1 the 15 actions called for by the Report.

Box 3.1 The 15 Actions

Action 1 "Address the tax challenges of the Digital Economy" identifies the main difficulties that the digital economy poses for the application of existing international tax rules and develops detailed options to address these difficulties, taking a holistic approach and considering both direct and indirect taxation.

Action 2 "Neutralize the effects of Hybrid Mismatch Arrangements" develops model treaty provisions and recommendations regarding the design of domestic rules to neutralize the effect (e.g., double non-taxation, double deduction, long-term deferral) of hybrid instruments and entities.

Action 3 "Strengthen Controlled Foreign Companies (CFC) rules" develops recommendations regarding the design of CFC rules.

Action 4 "Limit base erosion via interest deductions and other financial payments" develops recommendations regarding best practices in the design of rules to prevent base erosion through the use of interest expense, for example through the use of related-party and third-party debt to achieve excessive interest deductions or to finance the production of exempt or deferred income, and other financial payments that are economically equivalent to interest payments.

Action 5 "Counter Harmful Tax Practices more effectively" revamps the work on harmful tax practices, with a priority on improving transparency, including compulsory spontaneous exchange on rulings related to preferential regimes, and on requiring substantial activity for any preferential regime.

Action 6 "Prevent treaty abuse" develops model treaty provisions and recommendations regarding the design of domestic rules to prevent the granting of treaty benefits in inappropriate circumstances.

Action 7 "Prevent the artificial avoidance of Permanent Establishment (PE) status" develops changes to the definition of PE to prevent the artificial avoidance of PE status in relation to BEPS, including through the use of commissionaire arrangements and the specific activity exemptions.

Actions 8–10 "Assure that Transfer Pricing outcomes are in line with value creation" include work on (1) intangibles, by developing rules to prevent BEPS by moving intangibles among group members; (2) risks and capital, by developing rules to prevent BEPS by transferring risks among, or allocating excessive capital to, group members; and (3) other high-risk transactions, by developing rules to prevent BEPS by engaging in transactions which would not, or would only very rarely, occur between third parties.

Action 11 "Establish methodologies to collect and analyse data on BEPS and the Actions to address it" develops recommendations regarding indicators of the scale and economic impact of BEPS and ensures that tools are available to monitor and evaluate the effectiveness and economic impact of the actions taken to address BEPS on an ongoing basis.

Action 12 "Require taxpayers to disclose their aggressive tax planning arrangements" develops recommendations regarding the design of mandatory disclosure rules for aggressive or abusive transactions, arrangements or structures, taking into consideration the administrative costs for tax administrations and business and drawing on experiences of the increasing number of countries that have such rules.

Action 13 "Re-examine Transfer Pricing documentation" develops rules regarding transfer pricing documentation to enhance transparency for tax administration, taking into consideration the compliance costs for business.

Action 14 "Make Dispute Resolution Mechanisms more effective" develops solutions to address obstacles that prevent countries from solving treaty-related disputes under MAP, including the absence of arbitration provisions in most treaties and the fact that access to MAP and arbitration may be denied in certain cases.

Action 15 "Develop a Multilateral Instrument" develops an instrument to expedite and streamline the implementation of the measures developed to address BEPS. Changes to the OECD Model Tax Convention are not directly effective without amendments to bilateral tax treaties. A multilateral instrument to amend bilateral treaties is a promising way forward.

The 15 actions aim at being inclusive and transparent in both their definition and their objectives:

3.2.1.1 Inclusive

The work on BEPS was carried out within the framework of the OECD/G20 BEPS Project, to which the eight non-OECD G20 Countries (Argentina, Brazil, China, India, Indonesia, Russia, Saudi Arabia and

South Africa) as well as Colombia and Latvia (who have started the accession process to become OECD members) participated as Associates, on an equal footing with OECD countries in the decision-making process, at the level of both the OECD Committee on Fiscal Affairs and of its subsidiary bodies responsible for carrying out the technical work.

Developing countries face issues related to BEPS, though the issues may manifest differently given the specificities of their legal and administrative frameworks. They have been consulted extensively and the engagement process has been institutionalized in 2014. The engagement has taken place via the Global Fora on Tax Treaties, on Transfer Pricing and on VAT; via regional networks in Africa, Asia, Latin America and the Caucasus in close cooperation with regional tax organizations; via the participation of the United Nations (UN) in the OECD's working meetings on tax through a Subcommittee on BEPS Issues for Developing Countries; and via the direct participation of the OECD Committee on Fiscal Affairs of 14 developing countries across a number of regions and different income levels.

3.2.1.2 Transparent

Consultation with non-governmental stakeholders was critical and several mechanisms were used to ensure that all stakeholders provided relevant input. Institutional engagement with business and civil society took place through the Business and Industry Advisory Committee (BIAC) and the Trade Union Advisory Committee (TUAC). Non-governmental organizations, think tanks and academia were also continuously consulted. Requests for input and discussion drafts were regularly published for public comments on the OECD website. Public consultations were organized to discuss the comments received on the discussion drafts and regular updates regarding progress of the work was provided by the Secretariat via webcast sessions streamed live. In total, the BEPS Project received about 1400 submissions from industry, advisers, civil society and academics, totalling about 11,000 pages of comments on 23 discussion drafts published. Twelve public consultations, streamed live, were held. Seven BEPS webcasts attracted over 40,000 viewers.

Stakeholders' input has been of key relevance given, in particular, the fast pace of the project. It helped to ensure that the measures were well targeted and did not unduly burden businesses with compliance requirements, while at the same time ensuring they were addressing the policy concerns that were the root cause for the BEPS Project. Stakeholders' input was also useful for identifying areas where "collateral damages" could have been generated. Importantly, a number of rules have been tailored so as to carve out SMEs when they do not raise the same concerns compared to large MNEs.

3.3 Delivery: The BEPS Package for Reform

In September 2014, a first batch of outputs were delivered in an interim form and presented to G20 finance ministers in September 2014 and leaders in November 2014 in Australia. The full BEPS package was approved by the Committee on Fiscal Affairs in September 2015 and delivered to the G20 finance ministers in October 2015 and to the G20 leaders in November 2015. It includes 15 reports, consolidated with the 2014 deliverables and an Explanatory Statement which describe the impact of the deliverables on the international tax environment and explain how the objectives set out in the 2013 Action Plan are expected to be met. The guidance following from actions 8–10 on transfer pricing has been consolidated into one report.

3.3.1 Bridging the Gaps Between Tax Sovereignties with New Coordination Tools (Actions 2–5)

Model rules have been developed and best practices identified to ensure that the design of domestic measures also takes into account what happens beyond a country's borders. Along these lines, a number of countries are already implementing the OECD/G20 model rules on hybrid mismatch arrangements (action 2). To ensure that the mismatches are eliminated even where a jurisdiction did not adopt the recommended measures, the rules are divided into a primary response and a defensive rule. These recommendations are intended to drive taxpayers towards less complicated and more transparent cross-border investment. Instruments such as the convertible preferred equity certificates or the profit-participating loans, which have been prominent in press reports recently, will not trigger anymore undue tax benefits.

With effective CFC rules in the countries where the headquarters are located, there will be less of an incentive to strip income out of other countries. For this reason, the building blocks of effective CFC rules have been identified (action 3). This will allow countries without CFC rules to implement such rules directly, and countries with existing CFC rules to modify them to align more closely with the recommendations. The outcomes of the work on action 3 also include fundamental policy considerations that need to be taken into account when designing CFC rules.

Best practices have been identified in the area of interest deductibility (action 4). A number of studies have shown BEPS occurring though excessive interest deductions, with both related-party and external debt, and have found that MNEs' strategic placement of debt and the associated interest deductions are sensitive to tax differentials and tax interest limitations. Indeed, a one percentage point higher statutory corporate tax rate of an affiliate than the average in the MNE group is associated with a 1.3 % higher external debt/equity ratio for that affiliate. The recommended approach is based on a fixed ratio rule which limits an entity's net deductions for interest and payments economically equivalent to interest to a percentage of its earnings before interest, taxes, depreciation and amortisation (EBITDA). The approach can be supplemented by a worldwide group ratio rule which allows an entity to exceed this limit in certain circumstances and by specific rules that address BEPS risks in the banking and insurance sectors.

BEPS will ensure that not only companies but also governments play fair and hence eliminate or modify preferential regimes that have the potential to attract paper income rather than substantial business activities (action 5). Participating countries looked at their own rules to ensure that they do not encourage or facilitate BEPS and have agreed on the "nexus" approach to evaluate whether preferential regimes on intellectual property (IP) are harmful or not. All OECD and G20 countries have now endorsed the approach which provides for a nexus between the location of the activities generating the income eligible to the preferential tax treatment (e.g., where the research and development (R&D) activities are actually carried out and where the expenses generating the income are incurred) and the jurisdiction offering this preferential regime. Transparency among governments is also a key element in the fight against BEPS, particularly in relation to rulings that have an impact on the taxable base of other countries. For this reason, a framework for compulsory and spontaneous exchange of information on tax rulings related to preferential regimes has been put in place.

3.3.2 Reinforcing Existing International Standards (Actions 6–10)

International standards in the areas of tax treaties and of transfer pricing have been updated and strengthened to ensure that they eliminate double taxation and at the same time do not generate opportunities for double non-taxation. In the area of transfer pricing, the guidance on the arm's length principle has been upgraded to ensure that what dictates results is the economic rather than the paper reality. What in effect is an anti-avoidance principle cannot and should not be applied to achieve the very results it is intended to prevent. The transfer pricing guidelines now contain a framework that makes it clear that legal arrangements are important and are the starting point of any transfer pricing analysis, but that at the same time the arm's length principle does not rely on self-serving contracts which do not reflect the conduct of the parties on the ground. The revised guidance clarifies how risks and risk-related returns are to be allocated within a group of companies, how returns on IP will be allocated, and provides detailed guidance on the transfer pricing treatment of synergies, location-savings and local market features, as well as assembled workforce.

Recognizing the difficulty in valuing IP, an approach for hard-to-value intangibles has been devised. The measure provides a backstop to otherwise possible abuses owing to the information asymmetry between taxpayers and tax administrations. The effect of this measure will allow the tax administrations to presume that a price-adjustment mechanism would have been adopted and as a result may rebase the calculations based on the actual outcome, imputing a contingent payment mechanism. New and more detailed guidance on the application of profit-split methods will be developed for integrated value chains where unique assets are contributed, such as those often present in the digital economy. Finally, simplification mechanisms have been developed in the areas of commodity transactions and low- value-adding services, two areas of particular relevance to developing countries and for which their contribution was paramount to understand what the concerns are and identify the best way to address them.

In the area of tax treaties, key changes to the Model Tax Convention have been agreed to ensure that treaties are there to eliminate double taxation, rather than being an integral part of complex schemes aimed at shifting income into no- or low-tax locations, often free of tax at source. The minimum standard in the area of treaty abuse will ensure that treaty benefits are only granted to those entities that are entitled to them. Once this standard is introduced in bilateral tax treaties via the multilateral instrument by the end of next year, the era of shell companies to claim treaty benefits will definitively be over. Further, a number of more targeted measures have been identified to address specific schemes aimed at benefiting from certain treaty provisions, such as in the case of dividend stripping schemes, dual-resident companies and hybrid entities.

The definition of PE has been modified to better reflect the business reality of today and avoid widespread circumvention of the principle that underlines it. The amended provision will ensure that a business's core activities cannot inappropriately benefit from the exception for preparatory and auxiliary activities, and that the PE status will not be circumvented any more via the use of commissionaires and similar strategies or the fragmentation of activities among different group entities.

3.3.3 Improving Transparency (Actions 11–13)

Work on transparency has focused on multiple fronts: transparency towards the public, transparency between taxpayers and tax administrations, and transparency among tax administrations themselves. Countries have worked collectively to provide a range of reasonable estimates of the magnitude of BEPS and its economic impact. Even if based on less-than-optimal data sources, the work shows that BEPS is significant and a serious source of concern in terms of lost government revenues. The work on action 11 describes the existing data sources and their limitations, provides for new indicators of BEPS behaviours and addresses the methodological issues and the approach taken in carrying out economic analyses of BEPS and of the impact of BEPS countermeasures. Recommendations are also formulated regarding new tools and data to monitor BEPS and the effects of BEPS countermeasures in the future.

Always in the area of improving transparency, recommendations have been formulated for the modular design of mandatory disclosure rules, which provide flexibility for country-specific needs and are based on the positive experience of countries that have introduced them (action 12). The report sets out specific recommendations for rules targeting international tax schemes. Arrangements which incorporate cross-border BEPS outcomes would be required to be disclosed if that arrangement includes a transaction with a domestic taxpayer that has material tax consequences in the reporting country and the taxpayer was aware or ought to have been aware of the cross-border outcome. Practical guidance has also been developed for the design and the implementation of enhanced information-sharing models for aggressive tax planning schemes.

The requirements for transfer pricing documentation have been substantially revised (action 13), with MNEs required to submit information regarding their global business operations and transfer pricing policies in a "Master file," as well as more detailed information regarding relevant related-party transactions and the amounts involved in such operations in a "Local file." An idea long supported by civil society has been developed and transformed into an international standard. Country-by-country reporting will soon become a reality and this has an extremely powerful impact on taxpayer's behaviours. In a major step forward in transparency towards tax administrations, the country-by-country reporting will provide a clear overview of where profits, sales, employees and assets are located and where taxes are paid and accrued. Guidance and tools to ensure a swift and consistent implementation of country-by-country reporting across countries were also developed, so as to ensure the widest possible dissemination of this information among tax administrations, while respecting the agreed safeguards on confidentiality, appropriate use and consistency. The first country-by-country reports are being filed and will be exchanged in 2017.

3.3.4 Balancing the Approach (Action 14)

As the transition phase will be critical and the risk of double taxation may temporarily increase owing to the introduction of new rules and guidance, it is now more necessary than ever to couple these measures with efficient dispute resolution mechanisms. Measures have been identified to ensure that disputes among governments on the interpretation of treaties are prevented and solved. The Mutual Agreement Procedure (MAP), the mechanism through which the competent authorities of the contracting states may resolve differences or difficulties regarding the interpretation or application of the convention, has been strengthened to minimize the risks of uncertainty and unintended double taxation. In this area, countries have agreed on a minimum standard which will ensure that treaty obligations related to the MAP are fully implemented in good faith and that MAP cases are resolved in a timely manner (within two years). It will also ensure the implementation of administrative processes that promote the prevention and timely resolution of treaty-related disputes. Finally, it will ensure that taxpayers can access the MAP when eligible. Furthermore, a growing number of countries are willing to use arbitration in their bilateral tax treaties as a mechanism to guarantee that treaty-related disputes are resolved in a two-year time frame.

3.3.5 The Overarching Themes of the Digital Economy (Action 15)

All these measures, and in particular the ones on PE, transfer pricing and CFC rules will also address the BEPS issues raised by the digital economy. Taxpayers will no longer be able to effectively establish structures that separate the income from the value-added activities of their business, a phenomenon that was particularly exacerbated by the key features and the business models of the digital economy. Importantly, rules have been devised to ensure that VAT is collected in the country where the consumer is located. This issue is particularly acute in the online business-to-consumer market and that greatly affects the level playing field between domestic and cross-border suppliers. The experience of countries that have already introduced simplified registration systems has been extremely positive and has had a strong impact on VAT collection.

In addition, possible technical options have been identified to deal with the challenges raised by the digital economy that go beyond BEPS. These challenges relate chiefly to the allocation of taxing rights among countries. The options include modifications to the exceptions from PE status, alternatives to the existing PE threshold, the imposition of a withholding tax on certain types of digital transactions and the introduction of an equalization levy. With respect to the exceptions from PE status, the rules for preparatory or auxiliary activities have been modified to ensure that businesses' core activities cannot inappropriately benefit from these exceptions.

The elements of the remaining three potential options could be combined into a new concept of nexus for net-basis taxation (a "significant economic presence"), with the intent to reflect situations where an enterprise participates in the economic life of a country in a regular and sustained manner without having a physical presence in that country. These options can then be discussed bilaterally by countries or be introduced as domestic law measures for situations where either there is no treaty in place or where the relevant treaty has been abused. However, they are not recommended as international standards.

3.4 Beyond Delivery

Delivery of the BEPS package is a fundamental but final step. There are at least three parallel and equally important items to deliver: implementation, monitoring and technical follow-up work.

3.4.1 Implementation

The BEPS outputs can be summarized as: (1) changes to the Model Tax Convention (MTC); (2) changes to the Transfer Pricing Guidelines (TPG); and (3) recommendations regarding models, best practices or building blocks of domestic law measures. Some of the revisions are immediately applicable such as the revised Transfer Pricing Guidelines, while others require changes to tax treaties, which are expected to be made through the multilateral instrument, and changes to domestic law, such as in relation to the work on hybrid mismatches, CFC rules, interest deductibility, country-by-country reporting, and mandatory disclosure rules, as well as to align, where necessary, domestic rules with the harmful tax practices criteria. The ball, in most cases, is (depending on the constitutional system) in the court of national parliaments as regards domestic law changes and ratification of international treaties.

3.4.2 Monitoring

It will be essential not only to support, but also to monitor implementation and assess the impact of the measures over time. This will include targeted monitoring of certain measures, including the measurement of the impact of BEPS and BEPS countermeasures, the proposed changes to Transfer Pricing Guidelines, the minimum standards on treaty shopping and mutual agreement procedure, the work on harmful tax practices (which will be extended to non-OECD and non-G20 countries, considering both legislative and administrative practices) and the implementation of the country-by-country reporting requirements, to be reviewed by 2020.

3.4.3 Technical Follow-Up Work

In addition to the work on the development of the multilateral instrument to open it for signature by 2016, some additional work needs to be carried out at the technical level. This includes finalizing transfer pricing guidance on the application of transactional profit split methods and on financial transactions, discussing the rules for the attribution of profits to PEs in light of the changes to the PE definition and a continued examination of the issues relating to the broader question of treaty entitlement of investment funds (other than collective investment funds, that is, non-collective investment vehicle (non-CIV) funds). It will also mean finalizing the details of a group ratio carve-out and special rules for insurance and banking sectors in the area of interest deductibility and developing a strategy to expand participation of non-OECD, non-G20 countries in the work on harmful tax practices, including the revision of the relevant criteria.

3.5 Concluding Remarks

The BEPS Project, which has been completed in just two years, represents the results of a major and unparalleled effort by OECD and G20 countries working together and with an increasing number of developing countries. The BEPS package represents the first substantial renovation of the international tax rules in almost a century. The jury is now out and it will not take long to recognize the important contribution of this project to a modern, fair and equitable global economy or else the failure of national policy-makers to look beyond their border and/or the next election.

RETRACTED CHAPTER: OECD BEPS: Reconciling Global Trade, Taxation Principles and the Digital Economy

Hosuk Lee-Makiyama and Bert Verschelde

This chapter has been withdrawn as Palgrave does not have the publication rights.

F. Boccia, R. Leonardi (eds.), *The Challenge of the Digital Economy*,
DOI 10.1007/978-3-319-43690-6_4

5

Federalism, E-Commerce and Public Finance in the USA

Michael A. Pagano

5.1 Constitutional Issues and Interstate Commerce

When delegates from the first states met in 1787, as required by the Articles of Confederation, many of the delegates believed that the current constitutional arrangement provided too few, if any, powers to a centralizing authority. The delegates began to redraft a second constitution of the USA that would clearly delineate those responsibilities of the central or general government as apart and distinct from the powers that resided with the sovereign states. Among the powers of the central government included the power "To regulate Commerce with foreign Nations, and among the several States, and with the Indian Tribes." In other words, while the federal government was granted the authority to regulate interstate commerce, state governments were explicitly denied the power

M.A. Pagano (✉)
College of Urban Planning and Public Affairs, Public Administration,
University of Illinois at Chicago, Chicago, IL, USA

F. Boccia, R. Leonardi (eds.), *The Challenge of the Digital Economy*,
DOI 10.1007/978-3-319-43690-6_5

to interfere with interstate commerce. Any action taken by states to regulate interstate commerce, then, would violate the Commerce Clause of the US Constitution and, therefore, be null and void.

In the twentieth century, states began to expand their taxing authority from a reliance on property taxes. Taxes on retail sales eventually became an important revenue source, such that, as of today, 45 states plus the District of Columbia (the seat of the federal government) impose a general sales and use tax on goods and some services. Each state defines what constitutes an eligible good or service for taxation—for example, many states exclude food and beverages – but most tangible goods are taxed by these 45 states. The US government does not impose a general sales tax or a value added tax.

States have jurisdiction over people and firms that reside within their own territory; therefore, they can decide on what constitutes taxable sales and on the tax rate for those goods and services. Moreover, local governments can be permitted by their states to impose a sales tax in addition to the state sales tax. As a consequence, there is no uniform sales tax rate in the USA, nor is there necessarily a uniform sales tax rate in each state. It is estimated that there are more than 9600 taxing jurisdictions in the USA with the authority to collect a sales tax.[1]

Sales taxes are collected at the "point of sale" by the retailer or merchant and then sent to the state for distribution to the appropriate taxing authority. A constitutional question arose when a state demanded that a retailer pay the owed sales tax revenue even though the retailer's operations were in another state. In 1967, a mail-order (catalogue) retailer located in the state of Missouri sold goods to residents in the state of Illinois.[2] The Illinois Department of Revenue requested from the retailer the appropriate sales tax, per laws passed by the Illinois legislature. The retailer refused to comply, and the US Supreme Court ruled that if the retailer did not have a substantial "physical presence" (or "nexus") in the state, the state could not force retailers to collect the sales tax as those retailers resided in

[1] Written Submission of Joseph Henchman, Hearing on Marketplace Fairness: Leveling the Playing Field for Small Businesses Before the Committee on Commerce, Science, and Transportation US Senate, 1 August 2012. http://taxfoundation.org/article/written-submission-joseph-henchman-hearing-marketplace-fairness-leveling-playing-field-small.

[2] *National Bellas Hess* vs. *Illinois Department of Revenue*, 386 U.S. 753 (1967).

a jurisdiction over which the taxing state had no authority. The concept of "nexus" implies that there must be a physical connection of a business to the customers of a particular state.

By the 1980s, catalogue sales had become an increasingly important retail activity, such that states were losing tens of billions of dollars in uncollected sales taxes. In 1992,[3] states argued before the US Supreme Court that it should abandon the "physical presence" test in light of the explosive growth in the mail-order industry. The Court rejected the plea and reaffirmed that a "substantial physical presence" or "substantial nexus" must exist for a state to impose a tax on out-of-state retailers, either for catalogue sales or e-commerce sales.[4] The Supreme Court further asserted that only Congress can authorize states to collect this tax on interstate commerce; otherwise, if states attempted to collect the tax without Congressional authorization, the action would violate the constitution's Commerce Clause, which gives Congress the power to "regulate commerce… among the several states."

5.2 Local Government Finance in the USA

General-purpose local governments in the USA include municipalities, counties and townships, all of which are creatures of their states and, as such, have legal authority to lay and collect taxes and fees for certain public services. In 2012, there were 38,910 general-purpose governments and 51,146 special-purpose governments, including school districts, potable water and wastewater treatment authorities and mass transit authorities.[5] Their powers, including the power of taxation and raising revenue, are derived from their respective states through enabling statutes. Because each of the 50 states is responsible for authorizing local governments' tax (and fee) rates and also for defining their taxable bases (e.g., although 45 states impose a general retail sales tax, 31 states exempt groceries from the

---

[3] *Quill Corp.* vs. *North Dakota*, 504 U.S. 298 (1992).

[4] Maryann B. Gall and Laura A. Kulwicki, "A Lawmaker's Guide to Sales Tax Nexus," University of Wisconsin-Milwaukee, Sheldon B. Lubar School of Business, 2012.

[5] US Census Bureau, *Government Organization Summary Report, 2012*. Accessed 22 January 2016 at: http://www2.census.gov/govs/cog/g12_org.pdf.

tax),[6] the fiscal architecture of local governments varies widely across the municipal landscape. Some states, for example, restrict the growth of the property tax levy; other states limit the growth rate of total spending to the growth in population; still others require all tax increases to be placed before the people for an affirmative vote.[7]

Municipal governments, or cities, account for 19,519 of the 90,056 local governments in the USA. The fiscal powers of municipal governments are quite extensive, such that nearly three-fourths of all municipal revenue is own-source, meaning that the revenue is derived by the fiscal authority of the municipal government. The federal government provides approximately 5 % of municipalities' revenues and the states account for around 23 % of all municipal revenue. Municipal spending, therefore, is supported by the city's authority to generate "own-source" revenue to a substantial degree.

Historically, municipalities relied extensively and almost exclusively on an ad valorem real estate tax. Until the Great Depression of 1929–39, property tax receipts provided the majority of municipalities' total revenue. Cities began to experiment with other forms of general taxation in the 1930s and 1940s, especially a tax on consumption called a sales and use tax. (A sales tax is collected by the seller and remitted to the state; a use tax is self-reported by the consumer of the taxable item and the tax is remitted to the government by the user.) At this time, cities also began identifying government services that provided a measurable unit of service (e.g., a gallon of water, a parking space) and charging the user of that service a fee. User fees in the post-World War II era grew rapidly as a percentage of municipal revenue.[8]

---

[6] Data take from the Tax Foundation, accessed 26 January 2016 at: http://taxfoundation.org/article/sales-tax-treatment-groceries-candy-and-soda-january-1-2012.

[7] Mullins, D. R., & Joyce, P. G. (1996). Tax and expenditure limitations and state and local fiscal structure: An empirical assessment. *Public Budgeting & Finance,* 16(1), 75–101; Mullins, D. R., & Wallin, B. A. (2004). Tax and expenditure limitations: Introduction and overview. *Public Budgeting & Finance,* 24(4), 2–15.

[8] For a discussion of the changing revenue composition of municipal governments in the USA, see Michael A. Pagano, "Creative Designs of the Patchwork Quilt of Municipal Finance," in Gregory K. Ingram and Yu-Hung Hong, *The Changing Landscape of Local Public Revenues* (Cambridge, MA: Lincoln Institute of Land Policy, 2010), pp. 116–140.

When property owners began to stage a "tax revolt" in the 1970s, the object of their anger was the rapidly increasing property tax liability. The problem, from the land owners' perspective, was that property values were growing very rapidly and therefore property tax liabilities were also increasing rapidly. Yet wages and income were growing at a slower rate. The tax burden on property owners, as a result, escalated. Citizen-initiated referenda at the state level and city ordinances began limiting the allowable growth in property tax receipts through a variety of mechanisms. Yet citizens continued to demand the same level of services. Consequently, cities turned even more to the adoption of user fees and charges. In 1977, user fees and charges accounted for approximately 30 % of total own-source municipal revenues; just five years later, user fees and charges grew to some 40 % of total own-source municipal revenue.

Today, the mix of revenues for municipalities is varied across the nation. Approximately 55 % of all municipalities are permitted to tax retail sales, while all cities can tax property (real estate). Even the income tax is permitted in a few states and about 10 % of all cities are authorized to levy an income tax. In the course of a century, cities' reliance on the property tax shifted. Today, 40 % of total own-source municipal revenue is derived from the user fee, 31 % from the property tax, 18 % from the sales tax and 11 % from the income tax. Yet only a handful of cities have the authority to collect own-source revenue from all four broad sources.

Because many municipalities have access to more than the property tax, the year-to-year fluctuations in municipal revenues vary considerably. Cities that rely on sales and income taxes to support their general services are affected immediately when the economy worsens (i.e., those taxes are 'elastic' with respect to changes in their underlying economy), while the fiscal health of cities that are dependent on the property tax change more slowly over time owing to assessment practices, billing cycles (which often reflect assessed property values from two or three years earlier). Data on cities' General Funds (the largest fund of US cities, responsible for over 50 % of total funding for city services) reveal that during the "dot-com" bust in the economic cycle of 2000–2001, sales and income tax receipts did indeed decline quickly, but property tax receipts actually

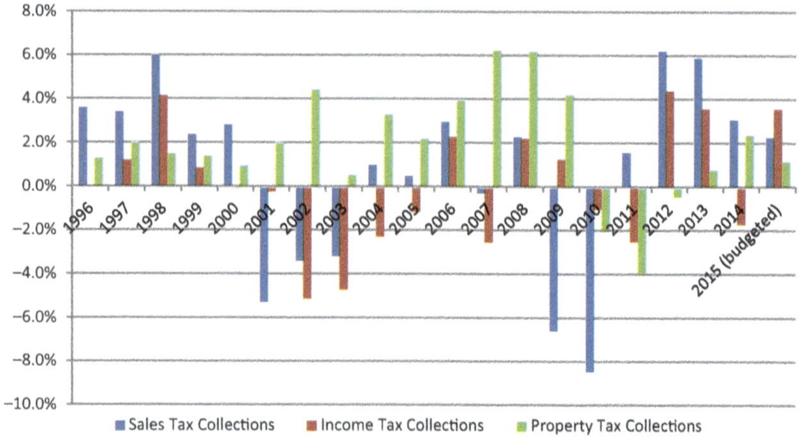

Fig. 5.1 Year-to-year change in general fund tax collections (constant dollars) (*Source*: Christiana McFarland and Michael A. Pagano, City Fiscal Conditions in 2015 (Washington, DC: National League of Cities, 2015))

increased over the recessionary period. According to the National Bureau of Economic Research, the Great Recession officially ended in June 2009. Yet the impact of the recession on city finances continued to be felt in 2010 and 2011, rebounding in 2012 (Fig. 5.1).

During the Great Recession, all three general tax sources (property, sales, income) registered year-over-year declines for four years before recovering somewhat in 2013. Nevertheless, municipal finances have not recovered to their 2007 peak. In fact, compared to the two previous recessions, the recovery has been much more prolonged (Fig. 5.2).

5.3 Sales and Use Tax Variations

When creating a taxing authority on consumption, states typically impose a "sales and use" tax. A sales tax is imposed at the time of transaction and at the point of sales; therefore, it is collected by the retailer. A use tax has the same value as the sales tax (that is, the tax rate is the same), but it is owed by the consumer or buyer of the good not by the retailer.

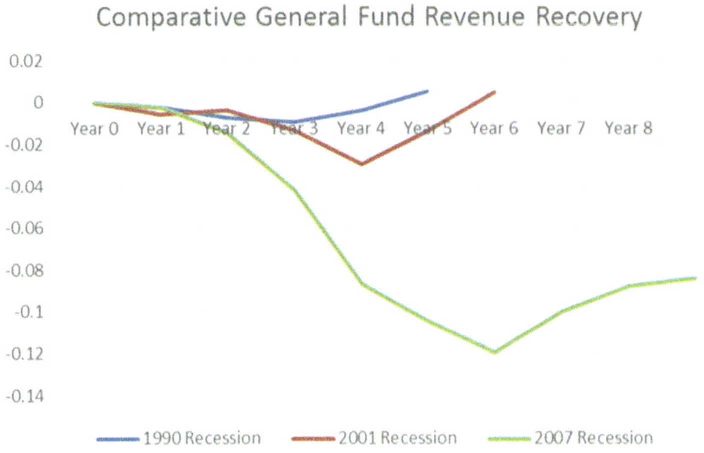

Fig. 5.2 Comparative general fund revenue recovery (*Source*: Christiana McFarland and Michael A. Pagano, City Fiscal Conditions in 2015 (Washington, DC: National League of Cities, 2015))

When a good is purchased from a catalogue or online through e-commerce, the buyer is required by the state to report the value of the good and remit the appropriate use tax to the state. In other words, because states have created a use tax, electronic and catalogue purchases are indeed subject to taxation by states even if there is no "physical presence" in the state and even if the electronic retailer does not collect the sales tax. This form of taxation, the use tax, is self-administered by the consumer and, by law, the use tax must be remitted to the state. Nevertheless, few consumers voluntarily comply on smaller purchases; many large purchases, such as automobiles, require a registration that can serve as a point of discovery and collection of the tax.

One mechanism for collecting the tax requires residents to include the use tax obligation on their state income tax forms. Of the 45 states with a sales and use tax, 38 impose an individual income tax and 25 of those 38 states also include a line on the income tax form that requires the individual to report the use tax obligation. The participation rate—that is, the percentage of income tax filers who provide information for the "use tax"—is well under 10 % for the 25 states with both an income tax and a line on the state income tax form requiring them to enter the value of

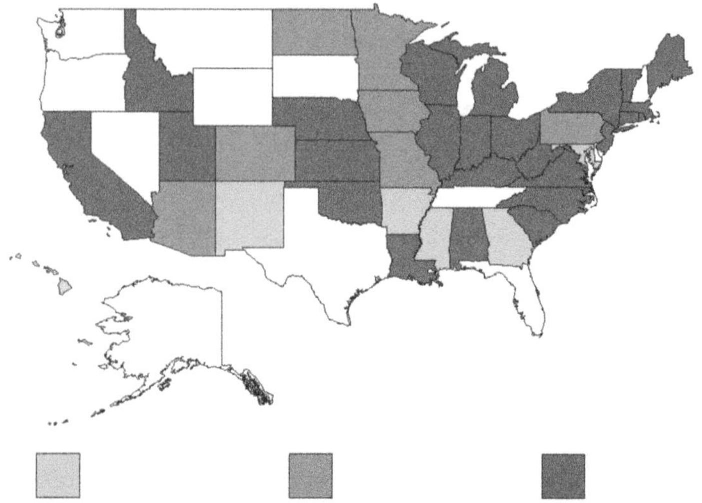

Fig. 5.3 States with use tax reporting on individual income tax return (*Source*: "Use tax collection on income tax returns in other states," Policy Brief, Research Department, Minnesota House of Representatives, April 2012)

the use tax. Fewer than 2 % of the income tax filers in 16 of the 25 states reported their use tax.[9] Moreover, some electronic retailers with no physical presence in a state voluntarily collect the tax and remit it to the state. By doing so, retailers make it convenient for the customer by removing the responsibility of self-reporting the use tax (Fig. 5.3).

In 2000, a Streamlined Sales and Use Tax Agreement (SSUTA) was prepared and submitted to all the states that had a sales tax authority. The SSUTA's mission is to simplify the sales tax and structure it on a destination basis so that states are better able to collect their sales taxes on remote transactions. Once simplification and uniformity have been accomplished, SSUTA intends to convince Congress or the US Supreme

[9] "Use Tax Collection on Income Tax Returns in Other States," Policy Brief, Research Department, Minnesota House of Representatives, April 2012.

Court to overturn the 1992 ruling so that vendors will be required to collect sales tax. According to the Governing Board:

> The goal of this effort is to find solutions for the complexity in state sales tax systems that resulted in the U.S. Supreme Court holding (*Bella Hess v. Illinois* and *Quill Corp. v. North Dakota*) that a state may not require a seller that does not have a physical presence in the state to collect tax on sales into the state. The Court ruled that the existing system was too complicated to impose on a business that did not have a physical presence in the state. The Court said Congress has the authority to allow states to require remote sellers to collect tax.[10]

Yet both "simplifying" and using a "destination basis" to assign the Internet taxes create challenges. Simplifying would require agreement on both the base and the rate for all jurisdictions within one state. For some states, that is, those with only a handful of governments with sales tax authority, that task might not be too onerous; for others, such as Texas, Missouri and Iowa, which have hundreds of jurisdictions with sales tax authority, it could be quite cumbersome (Fig. 5.4).

Destination basis, rather than point of sale, could damage the financial capacity of cities that rely heavily on the sales tax to fund general services, especially when the customers do not live in the jurisdiction. In this case, the seller would remit the tax revenue to another city government where the customer lives rather than to the city government where the seller is located.

5.4 Economic Impact of Uncollected Retail Sales Tax Due to E-Commerce

Because the US government does not impose a sales tax or a value-added tax, lost revenue to the federal government due to non-collection of Internet commerce is negligible. Estimated loss to state and local governments, on the other hand, is considerable but also difficult to calculate.

[10] Statement can be found on the Streamlined Sales Tax Governing Board, http://www.streamlinedsalestax.org/index.php?page=About-Us.

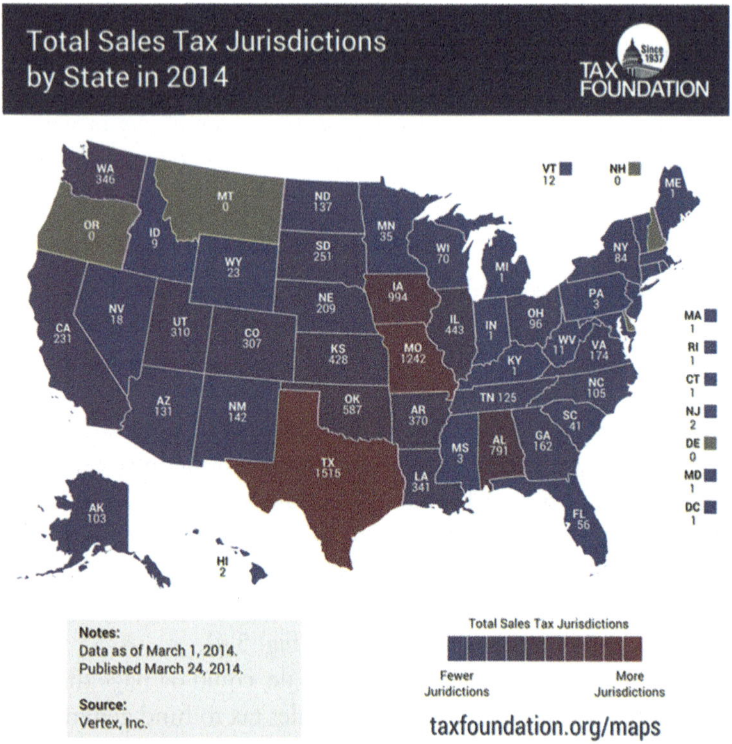

Fig. 5.4 Total sales tax jurisdictions by state in 2014 (*Source*: Tax Foundation, http://taxfoundation.org/blog/state-sales-tax-jurisdictions-approach-10000. Accessed 12 April 2015. Courtesy of the Tax Foundation).

Because each state regulates its own sales tax rate, defines its own taxable base and allows or disallows its local governments to impose a sales tax, the estimates of lost sales tax revenue owing to electronic sales are complex. Moreover, many electronic sales *are* taxed. For example, if a business has a "physical presence" in the state, the customer is required to pay the sales tax to the remote seller, which in turn remits the sales tax receipts to the state and, if the local government (e.g., a municipality) levies a sales tax, also to the city where the customer resides. For example, one of the largest retail department store in the USA, Macy's, has a physical presence—a bricks-and-mortar store—in most states. Therefore, when a customer makes a purchase electronically, the invoice includes the sales

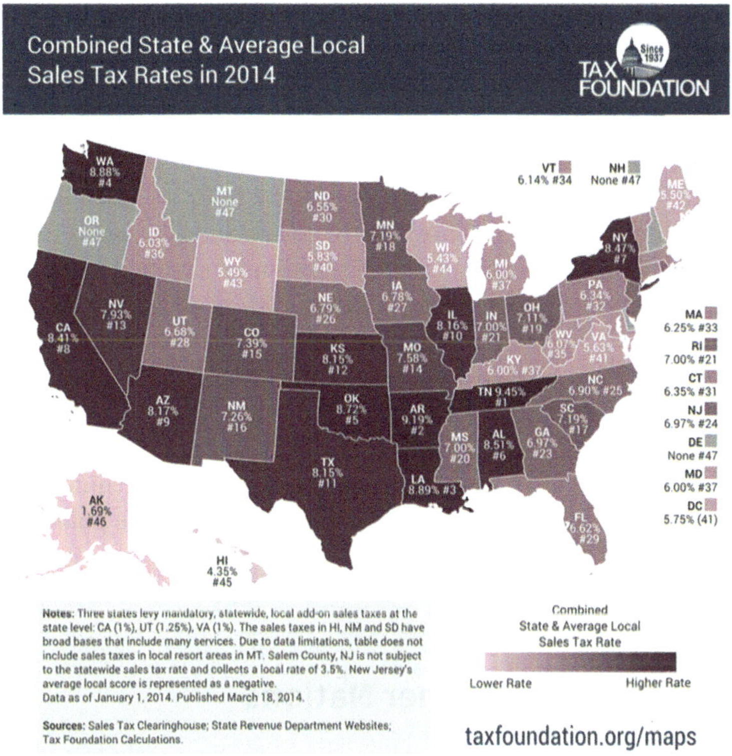

Fig. 5.5 Combined state & average local sales tax rates in 2014 (*Source*: Tax Foundation, http://taxfoundation.org/blog/combined-state-and-average-local-sales-tax-rates. Accessed 12 April 2015. Courtesy of the Tax Foundation).

tax owed to the state as well as the sales tax owed to any other local government with the authority to levy the sales tax. Other businesses, such as Amazon.com, do not have a physical presence in every state. Invoices from these retailers will or will not include the sales tax liability, depending on whether or not a "physical presence" (e.g., an Amazon facility) can be determined (Fig. 5.5).

Owing to the difficulty in estimating the loss of sales tax revenue as a result of e-commerce, few research studies have been undertaken. The most comprehensive research study is now six years old and it estimates that state and local sales tax losses could have been as much as $11–12 billion in 2012.[11] The losses of state and local sales and use tax revenue vary by state, with the largest states, such as California, New York, and Texas, losing the most ($2.1 billion, $960 million and $966 million, respectively). When measured as a percentage of total sales and use taxes that are collected by states, approximately the equivalent value of 4.25 % of total sales and use tax revenue collected by the states are lost and not collectible. The states with the most relative loss include Louisiana (6.56 %), Illinois (6.1 %) and Nevada (5.56 %). Although significant, the relative impact is slightly less for California (5.17 %), New York (4.87 %) and Texas (3.30 %).

The $12 billion estimated loss to state and local governments is a result of the US Supreme Court's interpretation of the Commerce Clause and its definition of "physical presence." The US Congress is in the process of considering The Marketplace Fairness Act which would require states to collect sales tax on e-commerce and remit the taxes to the home state of the buyer. The fate of the bill, which was introduced more than two years ago, is uncertain.

5.5 Lessons for Other Nations

The Constitution of the United States created a federal structure that delegated to the general government powers that are enumerated in Article 1, Section 8. All other powers, according to the 10th Amendment to the Constitution, are reserved to the states or to the people. Over time, states and localities designed their own fiscal systems, creating a heterogeneous system of taxation across the 50 states and the 90,056 local governments within the states. Each state is responsible for regulating business within its borders, but only the federal government in Washington, DC, has the authority to regulate commerce between and among the several states.

[11] Donald Bruce, William Fox, and LeAnn Luna, "State and Local Government Sales Tax Revenue Losses from electronic Commerce," University of Tennessee, 13 April 2009. The estimate has been challenged in another report, reducing it to approximately $4 billion; see Empiris LLC, Jeffrey A. Eisenach and Robert E Litan, Uncollected Sales Tax on Electronic Commerce: A Reality Check (2010). https://netchoice.org/wp-content/upload/eisenach-litan-e-commerce-taxes.pdf.

Until the advent of e-commerce, one of the most poignant challenges to the federal government's authority to regulate interstate taxation came from catalogue sales. When a catalogue company had no physical presence in a state, the state could not collect sales tax from its residents who purchased goods from the catalogue. The Supreme Court disallowed a state from taxing a firm that resided in another state. Today, and for the last 20 years, the volume of transactions with remote vendors has increased substantially, and much of it has moved to the world of e-commerce. The same ruling by the US Supreme Court that halted interstate taxation of catalogue sales also halts taxation on e-commerce sales unless a "substantial nexus" can be demonstrated.

To require remote vendors to collect a consumption tax and remit it to the state of the purchaser necessitates states to either work together collaboratively, which is exceedingly difficult given the diverse sales tax structures (both base and rate are defined differently by each state), or to engage the federal government to force collection. Harmonizing the sales tax rate across all jurisdictions in a nation is much less difficult when the number of participating governments is small.[12]

The complexity in coordinating the transfer of sales taxes throughout the federal system in the USA today makes the tax on e-commerce a challenging implementation issue. Moreover, the complexity becomes even more challenging as states and local governments that currently do not impose a sales tax consider such options in the future. Local and state governments also continue to adjust the sales tax rate as well as the sales tax base. As more governments adopt a sales tax, as legislative bodies continue to broaden the sales tax base (e.g., the inclusion of services) and as elected officials adjust the sales tax rate, the implementation of a mechanism that is fair and efficient in collecting and distributing sales tax receipts will become a political and administrative hurdle, possibly a barrier, to addressing e-commerce issues.

Even in the face of complexity, however, fairness demands that the e-commerce tax issue be addressed. As more consumers migrate to the

[12] Douglas Huenink, "Eliminating the E-Commerce Sales Tax Advantage in the United States by Following in the Footsteps of the European Union," *Wisconsin International Law Journal* vol. 31, no.1 (2013): 65–89.

Internet for purchases, uncollected sales (and use) taxes continue to grow, shifting the burden of financing public services to other segments of society. The charge, then, is to ensure that a state's fiscal architecture is fair, efficient, adequate and collectible and that it supports the government's service-delivery responsibilities.

6

A Few Ideas for Reforming Internet Taxation

Antonio Uricchio

6.1 Introduction

The history of humanity has often been marked by significant changes resulting from inexorable forces that are largely dependent on knowledge and innovation. Following some great discoveries such as the steam engine and electricity, the old feudal economy was destroyed, giving way to big industry and property rights, which greatly changed our approach towards human nature, politics and governments, in terms of the social contract and the way of living. Following the Industrial Revolution and the Ford-Taylor organizational models, the value chain, initially built around land, moved towards other productive factors such as labour and capital goods. Tax laws also gradually transformed the tax models by downplaying the tax on land and promoting the taxation of intangible assets (business, capital and labour income) which are personal and territorially fixed.

A. Uricchio (✉)
University of Bari Aldo Moro, Bari, Italy

F. Boccia, R. Leonardi (eds.), *The Challenge of the Digital Economy*,
DOI 10.1007/978-3-319-43690-6_6

The end of the twentieth century and the beginning of the new millennium appear to be characterized by the transition from industrialism to digitalization as a consequence of the diffusion of new technologies (Internet, satellite communication networks and so on) which, on the one hand, are adequate for representing the new forms of wealth, and on the other, are able to move, without specific problems, financial wealth around the world (even enormous amounts of capital can be transferred by means of the Internet).

During the last few years, new technologies, as well as the change in wealth production processes, have modified the way in which the real market is considered and perceived. It has shifted from a place where the exchange of proprietary rights took place, according to the interaction of spontaneous forces such as supply and demand, to a digital one that is considered to be an open environment without any borders and always connected—easily and/or freely accessible for the exchange of information, goods and the right of use. The discovery, the use and the diffusion of the Internet (the abbreviation for interconnected networks) have in fact created a world-wide web of open-access instruments through which wealth is transferred and produced and through which a vast series of potentially informative contents can be exchanged which are nevertheless relevant from an economic point of view. Therefore, the continuous and hectic process of technological evolution in computer science implies deep changes in the production and circulation of wealth. The development of information technology has given a remarkable impulse to dematerialization of wealth, thus reducing its tangible dimension.[1]

The new digital economy operates, therefore, with a different modality from market capitalism because the network connects an infinite number of subjects in a very quick and continuous manner on a twenty-four hours a day and seven days a week basis. As evidenced in the Jeremy Rifkin's study,[2] the Web gradually replaces the markets and introduces

[1] According to S. Cipollina (*I confini giuridici del tempo presente. Il caso del diritto fiscale* (Giuffrè, 2003), p. 286), the expression "dematerialized wealth" (*ricchezza dematerializzata*) has an empirical descriptive nature and may thus not be used for categorization purposes, whereas the more general term "intangibility" (*intangibilità*) can.

[2] J. Rifkin, *The Age Of Access: The New Culture of Hypercapitalism, Where All of Life Is a Paid-For Experience* (New York: Penguin, 2001). According to the Rifkin, "In the hypercapitalist economy,

accesses which create the possibility of using services, culture, information, relations and wealth, and of connecting and entering this reality and playing a role in some way in what has substituted the tangible assets for intangible ones, via a service provider that has substituted the traditional relationship between the buyer and the seller.

It is therefore clear how these manifestations of wealth can assume a new and different role and are less easily linked to a definite spatial dimension. Contrary to the definition of wealth in the past (i.e., in the feudal, industrial and post-industrial economies) which was represented by taxable material, physically perceivable, easily measurable (by means of conventional instruments such as property certification or accounting methods) and localized (considering the tangible connection to the territory), wealth derived from the digital economy is delineated as intangible and less subject to control, consisting largely of a flow of information to which the financial data is connected (the so-called *weightless economy*). The industrial society had strong territorial roots, needing physical structures for production (factories) and employing workers living in the area. On the contrary, the information society, owing to its nature, is intolerant of spatial limits, as it does not need material and physical structures but rather electronic nets and interconnections. The use of such instruments allows not only new forms of wealth to emerge, but also the circulation of capital and goods which are transformed into a dematerialized, virtual and random dimension (e.g., derivatives and financial flows). The digital revolution and globalization have determined the development of capital markets and financial economics and a reduction of the real economy.

The extent of this phenomenon can easily be understood by looking at a recent study by the Italian Association for Information Technology (Assinform). Compared to the worldwide real economy which grew by 3.2 % in 2012 with respect to the previous year, the digital economy grew by 5.2 %, covering almost 6 % of the world GDP. The same study shows that in Europe the average growth rate of GDP is +0.6 %, while

buying things in markets and owning property become outmoded ideas, while 'just-in-time' access to nearly every kind of service, through vast commercial networks operating in cyberspace, becomes the norm. We increasingly pay for the experience of using things—in the form of subscriptions, memberships, leases, and retainers—rather than for the things themselves."

the digital economy has reached 6.8 % of the European GDP. In the same period, the real economy in Italy dropped by −2.4 %, while the web market represented 4.9 % of the national GDP with a value of 68,141 million euros. Analysing the data, digital advertising, online gambling and e-commerce (especially high-tech products, tourism, and so on) are the areas that perform best.

6.2 The Impact of the Internet

According to the Internet Economy Outlook 2012 analysis, carried out by the OECD, up to 13 % of the revenue generated by enterprises could be attributed to the web, while this sector absorbed 50 % of all *venture capital* operations in 2011. As well as a direct contribution, the Internet has an important indirect effect on GDP, especially for the so-called "ROPO effect" (Research Online, Purchase Offline). This consumer behaviour has become part of our daily habits in that we buy using traditional channels after having identified and assessed the various options on the Web. Some studies have demonstrated that the ROPO effect has had a considerable impact on many traditional sectors. For example, 46 % of real estate contracts, in 2010, for a value of 26 billion euros, originated and were supported by the Web; 10 % of mortgages, for more than 4 billion euros, were granted with some kind of support from the Web; and almost half of tourism and travel-related services are bought on the Web. The cumulative ROPO effect in Italy for 2010 is estimated at about 20 billion euros.

To this we should add the entrepreneurs who use the Web to reach a higher number of consumers, consequently earning more and saving on various costs (i.e., in the display of goods, sales assistant costs, transport and postage costs). According to a study entitled *The Internet Factor*, carried out by the Boston Consulting Group, online enterprises (large or small) sell, employ, export and are more productive than those not online. The active online enterprises have registered an increase of 1.2 % in profits in the last three years compared to a decrease of 4.5 % of those offline and show an incidence of foreign sales of 15 % as compared to 4 % of those offline.

The Internet, by allowing an easier acquisition and circulation of information, experiences and knowledge among its users (entrepreneurs and private and public administrations), and by promoting dialogue and communication (chat lines, e-mails, Facebook and other social networks), allows everyone to gain some advantage and utility, which can be assessed economically or at least through cutting costs. In other words, accessing and surfing the net, together with the possibility of storing, analysing and transmitting information, experiences and knowledge in an interactive manner—as well as obviously, selling goods or offering services—appear to be capable of creating earning capacity susceptible to different kinds of existing or new taxes. From what we have observed it is evident that information technology significantly influences the forms and modality of the production and circulation of wealth, giving a remarkable impulse to dematerialization—i.e. loss of its tangibility. This can thus not be considered fiscally irrelevant for the law,[3] or neutral, or a mere instrument or technique, or at least a virtual phenomenon not involving physical events. Cyberspace cannot be considered a non-place, as not territorially rooted,[4] nor, from a tax perspective, a no-tax land.[5] The widespread idea that the Internet is only an instrument or method by which computers are connected and through which they receive and transmit electronic impulses, and that it is unsuitable to be disciplined by tax regulation, is unacceptable.

This phase seems to have been overcome; in fact, not only is the Internet presently very widely diffused, but it also seems to behave like a limited space if one considers the enormous quantity of information available on the Web, some of which is not very useful and often not appreciated (so-called junk information), and the number of interconnections, sometimes so high as to cause overloading of the Web. The need to end the "tax moratorium," which was required in the 1990s to promote the

[3] P. Costanzo, *Internet (diritto pubblico)*, in Digesto (disc. pubb.), vol. 1, UTET, 2000, p. 347.

[4] N. Irti, see n.9 below, p. 65, suggested that the web is non-space, because it is a non-place, being neither earth, nor sea, nor air. According to P. Cerina (*Il problema della legge applicabile*, in E. Tosi (ed.), I *problemi giuridici di Internet. Dall'e-commerce all'e-business* (Giuffrè, 2003), p. 739), despite the absence of an effective territorial link, the Web could be deemed as being related to specific places on earth.

[5] J.S. Gilmore III, No Internet tax. A proposal submitted to the policies & options Paper of the advisory commission on electronic commerce, in http:// www.ecommercecommission.org.

diffusion and widespread use of the Internet, is evident, considering the very high number of users and accesses to the Web. One may consider it high time to establish and apply new forms of levy directed towards the various forms of wealth generated by the Web, creating a new Internet fiscal framework and restoring equity to the tax system.

This awareness seems to be fully appreciated both at the Italian and at the European level, after the direct and indirect VAT provisions on e-commerce as set out by the EU directives and, as from 2015, the provision of special tax regulations that were studied by a group of independent experts appointed by the European Commission.[6] The 2014 Italian Budget Law established measures to regulate certain fiscal obligations, such as the purchase of online advertising services, of all subjects with Italian VAT registration.

As correctly claimed by Francesco Boccia in Chapter 1 above, taxation of the digital economy, of the e-commerce of both goods and services and of the purchase of "search" advertising must be completely reconsidered. Today, we face a distortion in the value chain in many areas and strategic sectors and it has become necessary to implement a new tax policy. The unprecedented level of tax avoidance and loss of cash flow is evident but the Web MNCs, with the support of some politicians, continue to oppose all efforts to reform the system.

We have to remember that the OECD reports (the first presented in 1996 and the latest in 2015) and the report by independent experts of

[6] As discussed in Chapter 3, the BEPS Action Plan identifies 15 actions to address BEPS in a comprehensive manner, and sets deadlines to implement those actions: "The spread of the digital economy also poses challenges for international taxation. The digital economy is characterised by an unparalleled reliance on intangible assets, the massive use of data (notably personal data), the widespread adoption of multi-sided business models capturing value from externalities generated by free products, and the difficulty of determining the jurisdiction in which value creation occurs. This raises fundamental questions as to how enterprises in the digital economy add value and make their profits, and how the digital economy relates to the concepts of source and residence or the characterisation of income for tax purposes. At the same time, the fact that new ways of doing business may result in a relocation of core business functions and, consequently, a different distribution of taxing rights which may lead to low taxation is not per se an indicator of defects in the existing system. It is important to examine closely how enterprises of the digital economy add value and make their profits in order to determine whether and to what extent it may be necessary to adapt the current rules in order to take into account the specific features of that industry and to prevent BEPS."

the European Commission have stressed the need to ascertain whether the existing tax levies are appropriate in dealing with an economy that is more heavily reliant on intangible and virtual assets,[7] or whether new concepts should be developed.[8] The question arises with respect to direct and indirect ecommerce, but also to any business activity carried out through the Internet, a place of virtual interaction. New concepts need to be developed to make the Internet a legal environment for creating wealth, rather than a mere instrument,[9] or, if an instrument, one that is organized.[10] Besides business transactions carried out entirely through the Web, one can perceive how information today easily circulates on the Web among all users (business, private consumers and even public administrators) with considerable savings.[11] From a tax perspective, this new dimension has originated new methods of payment, addressed by new levies related to licences and public services concerning the Web. Such levies show a strong ability to change and are the objective of this chapter, which aims at stimulating the scientific debate on their analysis.

In an attempt to overcome the impasse caused by the so-called Web Tax moratorium,[12] and to look beyond the dominant programme (too often conditioned by those holding economic power), two different approaches are possible:

---

[7] V. Ficari (*Regime fiscale delle transazioni telematiche*, in Rassegna Tributaria, 2003, p. 870) supports the existing rules, though suggests a shift towards a tax for the new economy.

[8] S. Cipollina, see n. 1 above, at p. 287, differentiates between the *revolutionary approach* and the *status quo approach*, whereas the former supports the need for new rules for regulation.

[9] B. Inzitari, *Contratti su Internet: aspetti della dematerializzazione*, R. Rinaldi (ed.), *La fiscalità del commercio via Internet: attualità e prospettive* (Giappichelli, 2001), p. 128. Against this view N. Irti, *Norma e luoghi. Problemi di geo diritto* (Cacucci, 2002), p. 66, and V. De Rosa, *La formazione di regole giuridiche per il "cyberspazio"* in Riv. Inf. e informatica 2003, p. 361.

[10] In this sense, P. Adonnino, *Il commercio via Internet e la fiscalità: gli aspetti generali delle attività transnazionali e nazionali*, in R. Rinaldi (ed.), V. Mastroiacovo, *Il controllo, l'accertamento e la riscossione dei crediti tributari derivanti da transazioni telematiche*, in Riv.dir.trib. 2004, vol. 1, p. 23.

[11] Products sold on the Web can reach a much wider range of potential consumers, thus yielding higher revenues for the economic operator, which also dramatically saves on various costs (including advertising, inventory, staff, agents and so on) and may result in lower prices with respect of sales to consumers.

[12] The tax moratorium, introduced in the USA through the Internet Tax Freedom Act moratorium was supported by international organizations (including the European Commission, WTO and the OECD) and various governments in the framework of strategies aimed at not hindering the development of the Web.

1. Hypothesise other levies that could be implemented in the near future—for example, bit taxes, taxes on the recording of Internet domains, on the licensing of IP addresses, on online advertising and on Internet accesses (hit tax).[13]
2. Adapt existing levies to meet the substantial changes which have occurred in the digital economy (VAT and income tax in the first place), in order to define, in more detail, the criteria to establish the levying supremacy of each Member State over the wealth produced through the Web by "stable organizations" or registered firms.

[13] During the mid-1990s scholars proposed the introduction of a levy on digital transmissions of information, called the *bit tax*, whose amount should be proportional to the number of bits transmitted and received. Conceived by Arthur Cordell and Thomas Ide towards the end of 1994, the bit tax was the object of analysis by the Commission of Independent Experts appointed by the European Commission for the purpose of drafting the Report *Building the European Information Society for Us All*. The Chairman of the Commission suggested replacing VAT on services linked to information technologies with a transmission-based tax, that is, a tax levied in proportion to the intensity of the transmission of information or communication. The number of bits or bytes seemed a sufficiently representative unit of the intensity of transmission and could thus be regarded as the (unit to measure the) taxable base.

Liable to such tax would be the person who owns the computer transmitting information on the net, whereas the place of taxable transaction would be that of the residence of the service provider. Consequently, the amount of tax due would be based on the number of bits transmitted, which could be determined through meters that each customer of the net should have installed. By contrast, the amount of bytes downloaded, as well as their private or business nature, would be totally irrelevant for the purpose of the tax.

Despite the important effect of countering information pollution, many have criticized this tax for having too loose a structure, attributing relevance only to the amount of the bits transmitted without taking into account their nature, the (business or private) transmitting taxpayer, or the type of activities carried out through the net. Furthermore, it disregarded the circumstance that a number of factors could affect the number of bits of each digital transmission.

In light of its features, the bit tax does not present a taxable event effectively expressing some form of ability to pay, thus making it inadequate to comply with a number of national constitutions in Europe. Although the inventors of the bit tax have compared it with the highway toll, the transmission of information cannot be directly connected to a public service towards the person obliged to pay it and thus may not be framed as a quasi-permutative levy.

From a different perspective, the bit tax would be unfit to replace VAT, taking into account the respectively different scope, whereas the bit tax would apply also to transmission of bits from persons that are not liable to VAT, thus significantly affecting a specific tax system having its own rational at the EU level.

Further problems would arise at the level of measuring the taxable base (for which a meter would be needed in virtually all computers) and for making tax assessment effective without unreasonable compliance cost or loss of the taxpayer's anonymity, meaning that the bit tax, as initially proposed, would create more problems than it would solve.

Despite solving many practical tax problems, we can't neglect many situations, such as online surfing, chats, online betting, online advertising, and so on. It would seem that the time has come to reconsider the tax strategy towards the Internet and to rethink whether new levies may/should be introduced with a view to catching all new forms of wealth linked to the Internet.

Of the two working hypothesises, the latter is proposed by the European Commission Expert Group on Taxation of the Digital Economy who welcomes the general consensus that the destination principle—that is, taxation at the place of consumption (according to them applicable for all goods and services)—be applied. At the same time, the group proposes to reconsider the concept of a stable organization bestowing relevance on the significant digital presence.

It is clear that whatever new tax policy is applied regarding the Web, or any extension or adjustment of the tax policies established for the real economy and adapted for the digital economy, such policy needs to be commonly shared by the international and European community. This is important not only because of the global nature of the Internet, but also to counter harmful tax practices such as tax avoidance, tax evasion and double or multiple taxation. It cannot be ignored that the unanimity rule, which applies to fiscal provisions, does not facilitate the adoption of new norms.

It is now time to overcome hesitation and uncertainties, and initiate a reform process that may result from a fruitful debate. The tax moratorium has, in fact, stranded the discussion on the Internet's taxation and led us into a sandbank, leaving a number of new forms for wealth creation still untaxed, or difficult to tax.

6.3 Conclusions: Possible Solutions

This section concludes the chapter by addressing issues related to four examples that, in the author's opinion, clearly show the current dilemmas of internet taxation and could give rise to new forms of taxation: (1) the recording of Internet domains, (2) the licensing of IP addresses, (3) online advertisements, and (4) Internet accesses (hit tax). It is submitted that, in all four cases, a tax would be fair, simple, levied on an effective economic event—showing the creation of wealth or the supply of a service—and enforced without giving rise to special difficulties or a high compliance cost, thus being compatible with the principles of neutrality, simplicity, efficiency and cost minimization. Furthermore, it is the author's opinion that the introduction of such new taxes would contribute to reducing the existing tax bias in favour of the Internet and make it possible to reduce the tax pressure on other productive factors, including labour.

6.3.1 Recording of Internet Domains

Internet domains are a proper key for income producing in the cyberspace and the Web market. Much more than representing a mere address, they identify the person owning them (a kind of logo, or advertisement instrument, to be used on- and offline) and detect online users connected to them. Recordings have been regulated by appropriate technical and conventional rules (so-called rules of *naming*) and special entities—acting at the international, continental and national level—have been entrusted with the competence of attributing domain names and to control recordings, generally on a "first come, first served" basis. In virtually all countries, registration problems have kept authorities and judges very busy over the last few years, thus leading some scholars to plead for the introduction of specific legal rules in this respect.

This result may be achieved by transforming the nature of registration authorities into state authorities who would licence the use of domains and more substantially control all possible related issues, starting with a different way of controlling the eligibility to register the domain. Accordingly, the authorities would not just ascertain whether the requested name for the domain is innovative, but also take into account a number of additional substantial factors, such as the ability to reflect the activity related to it and so on. The authorities could therefore also be given the power to protect effectively the improper use of brands, signs and names, based on the declarations for the so-called netiquette (*net etiquette*), and, even better, serve as arbitration courts for the settlement of potential conflicts.

Characterizing domain recording as a public service would also make it possible to levy a tax on the registration of a domain to the person who requested it. The tax could apply at different rates,[14] corresponding to the nature of the activity (business, artistic, professional, institutional, employment and so on) or of the person requesting the registration (individual, partnership, company or other legal entity, public administrator) and pursue also non-fiscal goals, such as, for instance, that of countering cybersquatting. Furthermore, its revenue could be used to finance the system of domain registration.

6.3.2 Licensing of IP Addresses

The communication between processors connected to the net requires a protocol of two elements, namely Transmission Control Protocol (TCP) and Internet Protocol (IP). TCP transforms information in an appropriate format for its transmission over the net to the addressee, whereas IP is a two-number code that identifies the receiving computer. Unlike domains, the IP address is a mere number, which needs legal protection against its improper access (and use), though without giving rise to typical issues of the enterprise's owned brands.

Since no message can be conveyed without an IP address, it is submitted that a reform of Internet taxation could introduce a new tax on the licensing of IP addresses. Such a tax would be easy to levy and assess, fair and straightforward in terms of determining the relevant tax jurisdiction.[15]

[14] Tax literature of various countries distinguishes between various types of taxes, including those remunerating a specific public service and those that do not and are mainly imposed on an expression of ability to pay. Because of its nature (remunerating directly a public service and lacking an expression of ability to pay), it is submitted that the levy on domain recording should belong to the former category of taxes.

[15] The fairness of a tax on licences of IP addresses would certainly be greater than one on modems (suggested some years ago by F. Roccatagliata and P. Valente, *Bit tax: ultima frontiera nella società dell'informazione?* in *il fisco* 1999, p. 5514).

6.3.3 Online Advertising

By 2016 it has been estimated that online advertisement accounts for approximately one-quarter of all advertising in both the US and EU which represents a significant increase from the 2010 levels which had not yet reached the one-fifth level of all advertising. New marketing techniques have been developed for online advertising which increase the volume of information made available to consumers, with a view to improving the persuasive effect on them.

From a theoretical perspective a tax on online advertising would be fair, since it would be levied on economic operators in respect of information that is directly linked to their activity.[16] Introducing a tax on all forms of advertising—including online—could thus achieve the goals of equality, fairness and neutrality that are important in avoiding possible distortions.[17] Such a tax could be levied on the basis of a number of parameters, which take into account the instrument conveying the advertising message and the number of persons it may reach. As for online advertising the tax should also take into account additional elements, such as the number of days of Internet exposure, the presence of hyperlinks, framing or metatags and so on. Besides its non-negligible yield in terms of revenue for the state, such a tax could also reduce spam and trash messages currently invading the net. Furthermore, it would be easy to assess and its control could be carried out through the ordinary search engines.

6.3.4 The Hit Tax

Websites have become an important productive factor for most business activities, often making intermediaries no longer necessary. The number of accesses to a website could thus be used as an instrument to detect indi-

[16] According to the Italian Constitutional Court (*Corte Costituzionale*, 16 July 1973, no. 131; *Corte Costituzionale*, 26 July 1979, no. 89), taxes levied on information messages of a mere ideological nature and without any business advertising element infringe on the freedom of thought.

[17] At present, Italy levies only local taxes on advertising messages, thus leaving untaxed the largest part of advertising (including that conveyed through broadcasting media). Introducing a general tax on advertising would also make it possible to overcome this negative experience and give the state some substantial source of revenue.

rectly the wealth of such business activities. The tax on Internet accesses to a website, or a hit tax, could be levied at very low rates on the person that registered it, varying according to the number of times that the website has been accessed. Such a tax would also meet the criteria of efficiency and simplicity in terms of payment and assessment. By contrast, its localization could be somewhat more difficult, though the criteria given by the OECD (see Chap. 3 on Base Erosion and Profit Shifting) could be used to overcome such problems.

In conclusion, the solutions to the problems generated by the new international digital economy are numerous and they need to be addressed as soon as possible. The nature of competition among firms operating across national and continental borders is significantly different from that of firms doing business within national borders. In other words, some are taxed while others are not, and this situation distorts competition in a completely unacceptable manner.

7

The Digital Economy and the Tax Regime in the UK

Robert Leonardi

7.1 Introduction

The UK represents the country in which the Internet has had the largest impact on GDP. It is estimated that, by 2016, the Internet will account for 12.4 % of GDP, up from the 8.3 % registered six years earlier. The turnover in the digital economy will reach 347 billion US dollars, and its impact on the UK economy will be second only to the property market. In other words, its economic importance for the country's economy has surpassed that of manufacturing.

Almost a quarter of the retail trade (23 %) is carried out through the Internet and that percentage is rising as more and more new companies are created to exploit the potential of the Internet or as already-established retail companies—such as John Lewis—adjust to the new competition by exploiting the option of Internet sales. The use of the

R. Leonardi (✉)
Political Science Department and School of Government,
LUISS University, Rome, Italy

F. Boccia, R. Leonardi (eds.), *The Challenge of the Digital Economy*,
DOI 10.1007/978-3-319-43690-6_7

Internet for purchasing goods is particularly strong in the clothing sector, but the use of the Internet is quickly spreading into other sectors, such as the furniture and sports equipment trade and tourism services. The Internet is particularly important for the latter, given the increased use of AirBnB, TripAdvisor, Bookings.com, Expedia, Trivago, Opodo and so on in booking holidays, hotels, air travel, car rentals and all other services connected with holiday travel.

The digital economy is fast becoming "the economy" given its impact on all economic sectors. We have mentioned above the role of the Internet in the retail industry, but it is also equally important in manufacturing through the use of robots and 3D printing in the production process. In logistics, digital capacity has become crucial to the ability to track the transfer of goods from one point to another, to sort out deliveries and to make it possible for deliveries to take place during the same day as the placement of the order. Other sectors that have been impacted by the Internet can be identified in the field of education with the enabling of remote learning by permitting classes, exams and evaluations to take place without the consideration of physical distance. The same is true in the field of medicine, where patients can be diagnosed, monitored and managed irrespective of time or the distance that exists between the patient and the doctor. Finally, there is the field of financial services, which no longer requires a bricks-and-mortar bank for deposits or transactions. Everything can now be done remotely through the use of a computer, iPad or smartphone. In the UK all these aspects of the digital economy are present, and they have had a significant impact in changing people's daily routines and social and economic interactions, more so than in any other European or Western country.

From the beginning of the digital age the UK has witnessed the strong presence of the top MNCs operating on the Web, from Facebook to Google, Amazon, Apple and eBay. Other important MNCs—for example, Starbucks, Hewlett-Packard and Yahoo— are present in the country,[1]

[1] The Chinese MNCs—Alibaba, Baidu and JD.com—do not have the same level of presence registered by Amazon or eBay. However, the size of Alibaba makes it a potentially important player in the European market. At the present time it accounts for 60 % of e-commerce in China. It covers services involving consumer-to-consumer, business-to-consumer, and business-to-business transactions. In September 2014 it launched the biggest IPO ever seen on the New York Stock Exchange.

but after 2005 it emerged that few of these MNCs had, in fact, paid any tax on their UK operations, thereby contributing to the erosion of the UK tax base and the reduction of government revenues for the purpose of financing essential government services. Another issue that has arisen is whether the companies operating in the digital economy are so successful because they offer services not provided by others or owing to the fact that in contrast to domestic firms they do not pay their fair share of taxes and therefore enjoy a financial advantage that distorts competition vis-à-vis domestic firms.

This state of affairs has prompted the UK government to take action within the context of the EU, OECD and G20 to find a response to the challenge of the erosion of its tax base. The response has been couched in an innovate approach to change the definition of the basis for taxation from the presence of the company in the UK to the turnover of sales in the UK no matter where the company is formally headquartered or whether it has a management facility in the country.

The issues involved in the discussion of how to respond to the eroding tax base are focused on: (1) the taxing of the sales and profits generated by MNCs in the various EU countries vis-à-vis domestic producers and retail operators; (2) the competition among EU member states in the attraction of company headquarters through tax moratoriums or low-tax regimes; (3) the formulation of international standards on taxation; and (4) the implementation of forward-looking tax regimes in cooperation with other important national authorities.

It can be argued that the debate on how countries should respond to the eroding tax base involves two considerations. The first is the role of MNCs and the lack of adequate policies on the national and international level in response to the opportunities generated by increasing cross-border operations. The second is associated with the role of the Internet in providing an effective channel of operation in advertising and retail sales through the digital economy. It is where these two aspects meet—i.e., MNCs operating in the digital economy—that the problem is particularly acute, given the increasing importance of the Internet in influencing or determining the outcome of competition between domestic and multinational firms and in the generation of profits to be distributed to stockholders.

This chapter looks at how the challenge presented by the increased importance of the digital economy is being managed in the UK, given that the country has the largest percentage of GDP involved in the digital economy and is also the country that has the largest presence of MNCs in its territory. In the past, the UK has attempted to attract MNCs for the purpose of benefiting from FDI in its economy and the generation of increased wealth and job opportunities. But, after the economic and financial crisis of 2008–2009, the presence of MNCs, combined with the digital economy, began to demonstrate some of the more negative impacts on government revenues and the ability to maintain a level playing field in terms of competition between domestic and foreign firms.

7.2 The Eroding UK Tax Base and the Challenge of Creating a Level Playing Field

It has been estimated by the OECD that the past regime that prevailed in the operation of MNCs and in tax avoidance excluded from national government coffers between 100 billion and 240 billion dollars annually. For the UK, the annual loss is estimated to be between 10 billion and 15 billion British pounds sterling a year. Government revenues have been hit significantly hard by the recession that began during the 2008/09 tax year. Overall taxes dipped from 500 billion pounds in 2008/09 to 485 billion one year later. During this period, overall taxes paid by corporations fell by 22.5 %, VAT revenues by 19.5 % and personal income tax by 7.7 %. This was also a period when the government had to take action to rescue the UK banking system from collapse in the form of nationalizations and bail-outs. The aftermath of these measures was to significantly increase government borrowing but also to increase expenditure to take care of laid-off workers.[2]

[2] The data are provided by the "UK Government tax receipts since 1963" Simon Rogers, The Guardian, 18 March 2013. The 8 October 2008 government rescue package for the U.K. banking system amounted to £500 billion. The major recipients were the Royal Bank of Scotland and Lloyds.

As suggested by the data cited above, the revenue flow generated by MNCs has been the most affected by the recession, and the level of taxation did not recover over the subsequent years. The reasons for this shortfall have been debated in financial and academic circles. It was unclear whether the lack of tax revenues was owing to lingering economic difficulties or to an aggressive policy of "tax planning" on the part of the MNCs to avoid the payment of taxes in developed markets through a series of measures and the transfer of profits to tax havens or countries with zero taxation on profits.

In taking into account the decline in the payment of corporate taxes, the UK government was particularly concerned with the level of corporate tax paid by "offshore" companies or those not domiciled in the UK. In 2011/12 the corporate tax collected from offshore companies amounted to £9.2 billion and one year later it had fallen to £5.2 billion with projections that forecast continually declining revenues over the following years.

Revenues generated by VAT have also not significantly rebounded in response to the increase in growth and in consumer spending experienced by the country since 2010. Where have the corporate tax and VAT revenues disappeared to despite the increase economic and commercial activity? The answer has been traced to the increased impact of the digital economy and the role of MNCs in the retail and advertising industries.[3]

To recuperate these losses it has been necessary for the UK government to rethink its approach to corporate taxation and the imposition of VAT. After the change in government after the 2010 parliamentary elections, the Conservative–Liberal coalition government began to reorganize fundamental aspects of the budget, from the reining in of government spending to a more effective approach in closing the loopholes that

[3] The issues involved with the payment of VAT concern three separate forms of transactions: (1) supply of electronic services, (2) supply over the internet of services other than electronic ones, and (3) supply of goods. The EU position on VAT stipulates the following: "The VAT treatment depends on the type of supply. It is also relevant to consider who the recipient of the good or service is—i.e. whether the customer is a business or an end consumer. This is relevant in terms of both the place of supply (country of taxation) and deductibility of VAT." Report of the Commission Expert Group on Taxation of the Digital Economy Report of the Commission Expert Group on Taxation of the Digital Economy.

permitted many companies to avoid taxation. In 2012 the UK began to place the issue of international taxation regimes on the table at both the EU Summit and the G20 meeting in Mexico.

The UK government's position at the two meetings was expressed by a government official in the following terms: "In recent years it has become clear that the international tax rules have not kept pace with globalization and most business practices which have led to some multinational enterprises exploiting the rules to pay little or no tax in many of the markets in which they operate." The differentiation in the treatment by the national tax authorities of domestic versus foreign multinationals threatened to heighten the difficulties faced by domestic manufacturers and retailers subject to national tax regimes versus foreign companies that operated according to a completely different set of rules.

Accordingly, as has already been discussed by Raffaele Russo in Chap. 3 the decision was taken to allocate the study of the issues associated with the evolution of the digital economy and international tax rules to the OECD—a neutral international governmental body—and to come up with recommendations for changes to be undertaken by the participating governments. The study was given the go-ahead in 2013 and operationalized through the creation of the BEPS task force in 2014. The task force was given two years to come up with recommendations on 15 specific aspects of the issues involved. The final report was produced in October 2015 and member governments have pledged to implement all of the recommendations by 2017 through the restructuring of internal tax legislation at the national and EU levels in addition to the reformulation of bilateral tax treaties.

What gives the process of studying and implementing new international taxation rules weight is that the driving force of the innovation is provided by the US government, on the one hand, and the European Commission and the Council of the European Union on the other. Countries on both sides of the Atlantic have been negatively affected by the tax planning decisions undertaken by the MNCs in the management of their cross-border tax policies and, therefore, they have become actively interested in blocking the continued erosion of their tax base. The EU is an active member of the G20 through the presence of the Commission and the Council in addition to the European Central Bank. In addition, it has created its own group of experts to monitor the activities of the BEPS study group in order to be in a position to immediately translate the OECD recommendations into EU provisions.[4]

The BEPS Project is also an indication of how, in the new era of the digital economy, it is no longer sufficient (and in fact becomes counter-productive) for national governments to act on their own. MNCs have the ability to shift their production, management and distribution facilities from one country to another with ease and unless the rules of operation change on a multilateral basis so that everyone is obliged to play by the same set of rules, the MNCs will continue to have the ability to avoid the payment of taxes.

A case in point is offered by the examples of the payment (or rather, the lack of) of taxes by four MNCs in the UK.[5] In 2016 the UK tax office, Her Majesty's Revenue and Customs (HMRC), arrived at an agreement with Google for the payment of £11.3 million for back taxes not paid over a five-year period starting in 2005—as reported by George Osborne during the period when Labour was in power. In comparison to the estimated profits made by Google and taking into account the dividends distributed to its shareholders by the company, the effective tax rate imposed by HMRC on the company was 3 % rather than the 28 % corporate tax that was in effect during that period.

Other examples of tax avoidance on the part of US MNCs operating in the UK are offered by the taxes paid by Starbucks, Amazon and

---

[4] In the EU Expert Group's Report the role of the EU in the G20 meetings is described in the following manner: "The EU is a full member of the G20. At finance ministerial level, the EU is currently represented by the Commission and the European Central Bank (ECB). At leaders' level, the EU is represented by the President of the European Council and the President of the European Commission. The G20 exerts significant and growing influence in areas of EU competence and where strategic interests of the EU are at stake, such as multilateral trade issues, regional integration, financing for development, combating the financing of terrorism or exchange-rate issues. At present, the European Commission participates in the G20 summits, the ministerial meetings, the meetings at deputies' level and in the G20 working groups." Annex 3, p. 60.

[5] The data presented by the Commission's Export Group Report on the Digital Economy shows for the 2011–2013 period that the five main actors in the digital economy outside of the USA—Google, Apple, eBay, Amazon and Facebook—all reported (and in some cases not reported) to have paid taxes on sales and profits in the lower single digits in contrast to what they paid in taxes for US transactions. This level of non-payment of equivalent levels of taxation took place despite having in many cases twice the level of sales and profits that were generated in the USA. See Annex 2A: Tax Over Income and Sales—Major Digital Companies.

Facebook.[6] The former has paid £8.6 million in taxes during the 14 years it has been in business in the U.K. Amazon, on the other hand, has paid £11.9 million in taxes in relation to a £5.3 billion profit. In 2014 Facebook paid only £4327 in taxes and even reported a pre-tax loss of £28.5 million despite the fact that it had paid its 365 members of staff a share bonus of £35.4 million.

All these cases offer examples of how MNCs are in a position to exploit the markets that exist in countries with large markets or in the opportunities afforded by Europe's single market. We have seen in Chap. 5 with the discussion of the sales tax controversy in the USA in which the residence of catalogue firms in different states to where sales take place has prevented the state in which the sale occurs to collect the appropriate sales tax. Without explicit legislation on the matter passed by Congress or on the basis of a specific ruling by the US Supreme Court this situation will not change.

A similar rule has been applied in the European single market. VAT has not been collected at the point of sale, and therefore the country in which the sale is made is not in a position to collect the usual VAT that is paid by all other firms operating within the individual country's national borders. In this manner, the MNCs are in a position to exploit not only their economies of scale and levels of technology but also their ability to hire a team of accountants and management experts in international tax regimes to exploit gaps in international taxation rules to their own advantage and, in the end, not pay the required taxes on their turnover in sales.

Thus, the challenge that needs to be resolved in tackling the avoidance of tax by MNCs is also linked to the parallel issues of, first, the existence of tax havens and, secondly, those countries permitting the holding of secret bank accounts. These two problems have been the object of considerable debate and legislation within Europe that have focused on the

[6] Accusations of tax avoidance have also been levelled at UK corporations such as Vodafone and TopShop which have a significant presence in the digital economy and retail sales. In both cases the shaming of the corporations' executives has proved to be a powerful instrument in convincing the management to take appropriate measures in rectifying their tax positions. This was the reason given by Google, Starbucks, Amazon and Facebook in cleaning up their public images in the UK and in the rest of Europe. In the digital economy the possibility of instantly communicating a company's tax position has become a powerful instrument in moving their executives toward a more favourable stance on compliance vis-à-vis existing national and EU rules on taxation.

struggle to open up the banking system in Cyprus, Luxembourg, San Marino, Switzerland and other smaller countries in Europe and abroad (e.g., Cayman Islands and Bermuda) and that have systematically used their banking rules to attract foreign deposits and corporate headquarters.

7.3 The UK Government's Response

This has been the challenge faced by the BEPS Project: to close the gaps in the international tax regimes and permit larger markets to tax the profits and sales generated within their territorial confines. For the UK government the controversy generated by the Google tax deal and the scale of tax avoidance revealed on the part of other large MNCs prompted the government to take action in anticipation of the results that were already evident from the BEPS study but which would not be finalized until the end of October 2015. Even more pressure was added as a result of the publication of the Panama Papers in early 2016 which revealed that a number of prominent figures in the UK (including the prime minister) were beneficiaries of secret bank accounts for the purpose of avoiding the payment of taxes in their place of residence.[7]

The UK government response has been underway since 2013–2014 in the attempt to anticipate the results of the BEPS process, to stem the public furry over the non-payment of taxes by large MNCs operating in the country during a period of recession and austerity, and to buttress the country's ability to collect indirect taxes on profits and sales taxes on goods and services sold in the country. The first step undertaken was to introduce the requirement for MNCs to report their country-by-country profits in addition to sales and costs incurred in the various countries in which they operate.[8] The requirement depends not only on the goodwill of the companies involved, but also on the transparency of the information reported

[7] In the case of David Cameron he was the beneficiary of the account opened by his father, but the account was closed before he became prime minister.

[8] This requirement should help in identifying those companies whose 'presence', in reality, is only a postal address where profits are deposited but where there is no other physical presence, employees or company activities, as was revealed in the US Senate briefings involving Apple and its complex system of subsidiaries and sister companies which are scattered around the world.

by the companies at the end of their tax years and in the ability to share this information among the various governments in the countries where the company operates. The legislation came into effect on 1 January 2016 and the first reports need to be filed by 31 December 2017.

The second major step has been the introduction of legislation in April 2015 that introduced the "diverted profits tax" that requires a UK taxable presence and the ability to identify when profits are diverted to jurisdictions that have no "economic substance"—that is, where in fact nothing is transacted or undertaken in relation to production or in the management of a company. In the past, a number of companies were reported to be located in Ireland where the tax rate was lower than the UK (12.5 versus 28 %) but even there no taxes were paid owing to the fact that the profits were transferred to other parts of the company for the payment of the rights to use the company's patent or to pay back internal company loans at exorbitant levels of interest. When profits are reported the tax rate will be 18 % but if the diversion of profits is discovered the rate to be applied on the profits will be 25 %.

The third innovation is the change in the focus of taxation on the place of delivery rather than on the source of supply. Thus, as part of the requirement for a taxable presence in the country, VAT taxes will be applied to where the transaction (i.e., sale) takes place. In the case of an Irish supplier selling in the UK, the VAT will be paid to HMRC and not to the Irish tax authorities. To come into effect, this provision requires the agreement of the EU and the other member states. Such a practice could help US MNCs to repatriate their profits to their home country owing to the "world-wide system" used to avoid double taxation. At the present time, the corporate tax in the USA is much higher—35%—than the one that operates in the UK. Currently, corporate tax has been pegged at 20% and it is expected to be reduced by one percentage point in 2017 and another one percentage point in 2020.

Thus, the UK has been careful in defining its new approach to corporate taxation in a manner so as not to alienate corporate interests in coming to or establishing permanent residency in the country. Since the 1990s the UK has been able to attract a good portion of FDI. In the 2014/15 period it was reported by the UK Department of the Treasury and Investment that the country had the highest FDI total of any country in the EU, and during that same period FDI flows accounted for the creation of 85,000 additional jobs.[9] Therefore, the UK has been careful to not create a potentially hostile tax environment that could make the country less attractive to the reallocation and start-up of new industries. For this reason it is important that all decisions regarding taxation be taken on the basis of multilateral agreements within an EU context so that other countries in Europe cannot position themselves in a more favourable position vis-à-vis foreign direct investors.

7.4 Where Does the UK Go in the Future?

The results of the EU referendum on 23 June 2016 have cast a shadow on the economic and financial future of the country. The reaction of the stock and currency markets has not been positive. In addition, the exit of the UK from the EU places into question its ability to work in cooperation with the other European countries in the implementation of the BEPS recommendations over the coming two years. The impact of the referendum results on the G20 and OECD context should remain the same, but it will have a significant impact on FDI and the asymmetrical position of the country within the wider European market.

Will foreign manufacturing firms remain in the country despite the changes in the trade relations between the UK and the rest of Europe? Will the large banks or law firms remains? It is difficult to believe that the UK will maintain access to the single market. As the president of the European Commission, Jean-Claude Juncker, stated on the eve of the referendum: "In is in and out is out." There seems to be little sentiment on the part of the EU institutions or in the original six member states to provide the UK with a soft exit or allow it to remain a member of the single market as is the case with Norway and Switzerland unless they accept the four freedoms associated with the free flow of people, capital, goods and services. In this eventuality, the UK will be more isolated from the rest of Europe and more dependent on being able to extract the maximum amount of taxes from the digital economy. In this manner, Ireland can no longer be used as a port of entry into the UK, and many MNCs will have to reconsider their positions in serving the UK market.

[9] UKTI, Inward Investment Report 2014–2015.

In the days following the referendum results, a new twist was added to the considerations of the Brexit results. The UK government under David Cameron insisted that it would not undertake to activate Article 50 of the Lisbon Treaty. That task was left to the Theresa May government that has indicated a March 2017 starting date for negotiations with the EU on the British exit from the EU and the single market. In addition, many of the proponents of Brexit have expressed the view that there should be a cooling-off period that will allow the cleavage between the Leave and Remain camps to heal, but most importantly to be able to map out the position of the UK government in its negotiations with the European Commission in establishing the basis of the ending of the relationship. It is not even clear whether the UK will in fact exit from the single market or assume a "Norwegian" positon of being in the single market but not in the EU. There is even the suggestion that before taking such a drastic step the UK needs to renegotiate its trade relations with individual countries in the EU and outside of Europe. Such a prospect may be supported by the Leave camp but it hardly will be the favoured option on the part of other EU member states.

What is abundantly clear is that the other EU countries and especially the six "founding fathers" of the Common Market want immediate clarity on the matter of how the UK will define its relationship with the EU in order to reassure the financial markets that the EU maintains its ability as a worldwide actor in financial and economic matters. If the UK delays in making its position clear, it may face the prospect of being pushed out of the EU institutions and single market by the other 27 member states.

The other question that needs to be clarified is the position to be assumed by the other building blocks of the UK represented by the Scottish, Welsh and Northern Ireland governments. Will they ask for a referendum in order to secede from the UK and can that secession take place prior to the exit of the UK from the EU so that they can remain integral parts of the EU? All these questions need to be clarified in the following months and years. The fate of the UK as a unitary constitutional system hangs in the balance.

It is still too early to determine whether the repositioning of the digital market firms will be swift or protracted. The UK will, most likely, take at least two years to wind up its relations with the EU if the other EU member states do not insist on accelerating the timetable for the decoupling of the UK from the EU. During that period the fate of the digital economy in the UK will be under scrutiny and many of the previous undertakings on the part of the UK government will be determined no longer by Parliament but by popular referendum, thereby changing the nature of the UK constitution from a parliamentary regime to a system of direct democracy dominated by the Web.

8

Conclusions: Taxation and the Future of the Digital Economy

Robert Leonardi

The chapters presented in this volume have highlighted the current state of the digital economy and its impact on the issue of taxation in the individual countries where the multinational firms that dominate e-commerce operate. They have set out the issues involved from the perspective of Italy is (Chap. 1), the OECD (Chap. 3), the USA (Chap. 5) and the UK (Chap. 7) and have discussed how the problems associated with the erosion of the tax base and distortion of competition within individual countries have led to the need to take immediate action. Chapter 6 discussed the impact of the digital economy on the national tax base in terms of being able, in individual countries, to maintain the adequate levels of welfare provisions that are common in Europe and the USA and whether the creative tax innovations engaged in by the MNCs represent a clear and present danger. In being able to avoid both sales

R. Leonardi (✉)
Political Science Department and School of Government, LUISS University, Rome, Italy

F. Boccia, R. Leonardi (eds.), *The Challenge of the Digital Economy*,
DOI 10.1007/978-3-319-43690-6_8

taxes as well as corporate taxes on the profits generated by the products and services that they are able to sell over the Internet, the MNCs need to be brought into line with the taxes applied to domestic producers operating in the market. In other words, as is clear from the OECD and EU studies conducted on the impact of the digital economy and discussed in this volume there is a growing presence of e-commerce, and up until now the initiative has been with the e-commerce firms operating across borders that have been able to develop a clear strategy of tax avoidance by taking advantage of the large European market created by the EU's single market and large nation states.

The rapid expansion of the digital economy and the explosion in the use of computer technology, the Internet and the increased flexibility in the use of smartphones and tablets have changed the nature of commerce itself. The dimensions of this change have been registered in relation to both the space and the time of where and when transactions take place. These leaps in the technology available to the consumer has forced national governments and international organizations to review the rules of taxation and competition between firms at an international level and to reconsider the basis of cross-border operations available to firms but not to national government tax authorities.

The digital economy has also been able to exploit the relatively recent changes in the world economy. On the one hand, there has been the progress made in the creation of a single unified market in Europe that incorporates not only the member states of the EU but also those affiliated with the single market as is the case with Norway and Switzerland. On the other hand, we have seen the creation of free trade areas in various parts of the developed and developing world in addition to the general reduction in trade barriers as a result of WTO's completion of the Uruguay Round and the attempt to bring to a final resolution the Doha Development Round.

As these dual changes in technology and trade relations have moved forward the same cannot be said in terms of the ability of individual governments or an assembly of governments to take into account the implications of such developments on their tax revenue bases, the sustainability of national budgets, the rules of competition applied to multinational versus national firms or the viability of existing practices in manufacturing and commerce. These changes have, in effect, changed the nature of market transactions.

Commerce is no longer dominated, as in the past, by the interactions characterized by the coming together of customers and merchants on the traditional "high street" within central cities or in the more recent "shopping malls" that offer abundant parking facilities for motorized customers capable of accessing large commercial facilities on the outskirts of metropolitan areas. Today, the commerce that takes place through the Internet has done away with physical space based on the presence of stores within or outside of cities. To make a purchase one does not have to be physically present within a store to browse the products or services on sale, or to select and pay for them in order to finally exit the store with the product in a bag or container or with a physical voucher certifying the purchase of a service. All of these various steps in purchasing the product or service can now take place electronically, and when a physical product is involved it is delivered by a courier service or in the case of a service the voucher is printed after the transaction has taken place.

In addition to doing away with physical space as the basis for the purchase of goods and services, the digital economy has also done away with time as a factor; the buying and selling of goods and services can take place around the clock at any time of the day or night. In other words, in cyberspace the shop is always open. It is not affected by employee contracts, working conditions, the weather or provisions for holiday leave on the part of its workers.

The elimination of these two factors of time and space has rendered a change in the nature of commerce owing to the fact that the enabling physical technology—that is, in the form of computers, smartphones and tablets—is accessible to a mass market around the world. As discussed in Chap. 1 smartphones are currently owned by a significant part of the population. One finds at least one computer in every home and tablets are widely diffused among the population. Even more important for the digital economy has been the ability to use these technologically advanced products to access the World Wide Web on a cost-free of basis; since the mid-1990s, the Internet has provided a worldwide system of intercommunication that has remained basically free of cost and free from government interference. Governments around the world have maintained a general policy of open access to the Internet, and the instances where this is not the case have remained few and far between.

Thus, it has been possible to access the World Wide Web on a relatively low-cost basis and as such it has become available to large sectors of the population: urban or rural, rich or poor, young and old. In addition, this new form of communication has been able to carve out for itself a conspicuous level of social status. It has become highly acceptable to engage in social networking via Facebook, Twitter and Instagram; to participate in blogs; and to maintain personal or collective pages for large parts of the population and especially for the younger generations.

As we have seen during the presidential campaigns (2012 and 2016) in the U.S. and in individual countries in Europe (for eample, Italy and Spain) the internet has paid a crucial rule in delivering the messages of individual parties. This was abundantly evident in the 2008 and 2012 presidential campaigns of Barack Obama in the USA or the Five Star Movement in the 2013 Italian parliamentary elections. The mass rallies that in the past brought together the candidate with his/her supporters and served as the principal mechanism for delivering political messages to those present have now become the mechanism for providing the primary messages that are subsequently communicated to a much wider audience of supporters and potential voters within national borders and abroad through the Internet via blogs, instant messages and targeted communications.

All these changes in the potential exploitation of telecommunication technology have been fully explored by a group of MNCs with a worldwide reach and which have been cable of taking advantage of the profit-making potential of the new technology together with open markets and tax havens in a combination that was not available in the past. These tax avoidance opportunities have become available to such a wide variety of firms and in such a combination of legal tax provisions on a worldwide basis. The de facto tax loopholes and tax havens have served to feed the interests of large multinational firms operating across borders and in large consumer markets. The relative ease of tax avoidance has forced national tax authorities to respond not only to the potential but also to the effective erosion of their tax base as we have seen in the case of the UK at the time that the country was going through a severe financial and economic crisis.

This differentiation in the tax position of firms has given rise to the application of different rules of competition between home-based firms and MNCs or between firms that are forced to pay taxes on what they sell and earn and those that are able to evade these taxes through a combination of creative avoidance measures that exploit tax competition among the various national governments in Europe and at the state level in the USA. This was the challenge that was taken up at the 2012 EU Summit and the G20 meeting in Mexico as discussed in Chaps. 3 and 7.

The question of how to approach the issue of tax erosion and firm competition was posed at the very beginning of the G20 process. The alternatives posed were to take a global approach through the UN, to take a regional approach on the basis of economic groupings—for example, the EU or the North American Free Trade Agreement (NAFTA)—or to introduce a functional approach focused on taxation involving the world's major economic powers. The latter approach allowed for a concentration of the participating countries in the G20 that included the major economies at the world level. In this manner, the G20 approach was in a position to create an international standard that could not be ignored or bypassed by others countries with weaker economic positions.

In the final analysis, the first two alternatives (i.e., through the UN or through regional free trade pacts) did not prove viable because, first, the UN does not have the mandate for taking decisions on financial and economic matters and trying to give it such a mandate would involve a long, protracted process of multilateral negotiations without any guarantee that the final decision would prove to be satisfactory in resolving the issue. The second alternative—i.e., operating through regional trading blocs—faced the same problem: mandate to operate on issues related to taxation and oversight of multinational firms. The existing free trade areas do not have the power to engage in such wide-ranging international agreements.

The third functional option based on the G20 remained the only viable alternative given that the combined bloc contained the major consumer markets at the world level and provided the management homes for the major corporate players in the digital economy. If these countries were able to arrive at a mutually acceptable decision and implement that decision through national legislation, then the rules applicable to the cross-border activities of the companies operating in the digital economy could be substantially changed in favour of those countries supplying the mass consumer base for the purchase of goods and services made available through the Internet. Otherwise, the countries that supplied the consumer bases exploited by the digital economy would be denied the ability to tax the transactions and profits generated by e-commerce in favour of countries—that is, tax havens—that contributed nothing to the production or sales process.

The choice in allocating the responsibility of studying the issue and coming up with a set of recommendations to the OECD was also of great significance. Over the past two decades since the beginning of the 1990s the OECD has been able to carve out for itself an important role as an organization capable of carrying out studies in an objective manner and in formulating recommendations for its members for the purpose of tackling common economic and financial problems. Given that it does not have decision-making powers and has as its members many of the important economic actors at the world level, it is in a good position to make recommendations that can then be implemented by its members on an individual or group basis. The OECD process represents an effective "open method of coordination" among member states that is effective owing to the fact that it is restricted to a few policy areas where there is wide agreement and where the members have a financial incentive to implement the decisions as soon as possible.

Now that the BEPS study phase has been completed and the 15 recommendations for individual state action have been published, it is up to each national government to implement, in a coordinated matter, the formulated recommendations. As we have seen in the case of the UK which anticipated some of the recommendations coming out of the BEPS Project, such government action is effective in changing the nature of the prevailing tax system and the response on the part of the MNCs. If not complied with, the new legislation threatens to subtract significant portions of the consumer market from the non-tax paying firms engaged in the digital economy to the advantage of competitors based in each participating country. Furthermore, in most cases non-compliance is not an option given the open nature of the digital market and the potential damage non-compliance can have on the reputation of MNCs. The years 2016 and 2017 represent the turning points in the interaction between the digital economy and the creation of a balanced level of competition and tax compliance between domestic and foreign firms. There is no possibility of turning back or ignoring the impacts that have been registered during the previous decade. The open nature of the digital economy and social interactions via the Internet requires that the dominant firms assume a role of social responsibility vis-à-vis their customers and vis-à-vis the countries in which they operate.

To undertake the necessary changes will require a clear institutional framework and a significant collaboration between the EU institutions and the member states. The vote for Brexit places into question what will be the role undertaken by the UK in finalizing a response to the conclusions arrived at by the OECD/EU studies on base erosion and profit shifting. Will the UK detach itself from the recommendations or will it cooperate in providing a combined response to the issues that have been raised? It is too early to tell, but the need to take action in 2017 is impelling.

As we have seen since 2012 the digital economy does not stand still. It is positioned to make decisions on the basis of the opportunities presented. What will be important is whether the BEPS recommendations will be implemented and how the digital actors will react given the unclear institutional framework that has developed.

Retraction Note to: OECD BEPS: Reconciling Global Trade, Taxation Principles and the Digital Economy

Hosuk Lee-Makiyama and Bert Verschelde

Retraction Note:

Chapter "OECD BEPS: Reconciling Global Trade, Taxation Principles and the Digital Economy" in: Francesco Boccia and Robert Leonardi, The Challenge of the Digital Economy, DOI 10.1007/978-3-319-43690-6_4

The chapter published in the book 'The Challenge of the Digital Economy', pages 55-69, DOI 10.1007/978-3-319-43690-6_4 has been retracted because Palgrave does not have the publication rights.

The online version for this chapter can be found at 10.1007/978-3-319-43690-6_4

F. Boccia, R. Leonardi (eds.), *The Challenge of the Digital Economy*,
10.1007/978-3-319-43690-6_9

Appendix: "Digital Economy: Facts, Trends and Developments"—EU Commission, Expert Group on Taxation of the Digital Economy

A.1 Digital Economy: Facts, Trends and Developments

A.1.1 Characteristics of the Digital Economy

The digital economy is the result of the transformational effects of new General Purpose Technologies (GPT) in the fields of information and communication. It has implications beyond the Information and Communication Technology (ICT) sector, impacting all sectors of the economy and society: retail, transport, financial services, manufacturing, education, healthcare, media and so on. Furthermore, the Internet empowers people by enabling them to create and share ideas, giving rise to new content, entrepreneurs and markets, as well as new opportunities for innovation and employment. The Group believes firmly that the digital economy offers great opportunities for Europe, including solutions and opportunities to radically simplify tax administration and collection. Nevertheless, the digital economy also poses new challenges to which our tax systems will need to adapt. We publish with the permission of the

F. Boccia, R. Leonardi (eds.), *The Challenge of the Digital Economy*,
DOI 10.1007/978-3-319-43690-6

European Commission the introductory part of the study conducted by the EU on the impact of the digital economy on Europe and the steps that need to be taken as part of the BPES process. The EU is a part of the G20 and has taken an active role in the discussions of what needs to be done to create the basis of fair competition between multinational and national firms operating within the digital economy. The study was finalized by the Commission on 28 May 2014.

Defining what constitutes the digital economy has proven problematic, because of the ever-changing technologies of the ICT sector and the widespread diffusion of the digital economy within the whole economy; it can no longer be described as a separate part, or subset, of the mainstream economy. However, it is possible to characterize it through a set of key features: mobility, network effects and use of data.

A.1.1.1 Mobility

The digital economy allows a new unprecedented level of mobility. Digitalization has made intangible assets more important than physical production; since a digital product can be replicated at almost no cost once its blueprint has been developed, the location of the development of this blueprint is where value is often created. Digitalization has allowed companies to reduce core business costs. Factors of production are more mobile; ICT-driven cost reductions enable firms to outsource many corporate functions to territories with lower costs. Digitalization enables firms to benefit from lower workforce costs per unit of value because many processes can be automated.

The geographic mobility of products has greatly increased since the cost of storing and transporting digital products is virtually zero. This enables companies to operate in markets anywhere in the world, exposing local markets and firms to additional competition. Tax authorities may see a reduction in tax receipts because indirect taxes are difficult to collect and the foreign producer does not have a presence for direct tax.

Digitalization has enhanced mobility between products; analogue versions are losing market share to digitized products (e.g., media content,

3D printing). The migration from ICT hardware ownership towards cloud-based ICT services has enhanced the mobility between goods and services. Consumers are increasingly able to access and utilize services for a limited period rather than buying outright. This blurring of the distinction between the producer and consumer (the "prosumer") could cause challenges for tax authorities since identifying producers becomes more difficult.

A.1.1.2 Network Effects

Digitalization pushes down marginal cost of products and an equal pressure applies to prices. New digital companies may have low gross margins on their products, and to be profitable they need huge scales of operation in order to cover fixed costs. Rapid growth to a large scale is a necessary feature of their business model which becomes sustainable thanks to the lowering of geographical barriers (as seen above). Since the room for competition in price is limited, the competition occurs in the quality and utility of the products, allowing price above marginal cost as monopolistic competition theory suggests.

New digital companies engage in a fierce race to innovate in order to create better or new product lines; small differences in quality can cause millions of consumers to switch, translating into potentially huge profit differences. This winner-takes-all model—where companies compete dynamically for the market (i.e., defining new markets through innovative products) rather than in the market (i.e., increasing market share)—creates monopolies and high volatility since these monopolies are highly contestable through innovation.

The winner-takes-all model is particularly visible in the creation of dominant platforms through network effects, whereby consumers enjoy more utility from a product the more other people use that product.

A specific type of network effect is increasingly prominent: the two-sided network, whereby two groups of users interact with each other—the utility to one group of users increases with the size of another group of users. All major digital players provide digital platforms (e.g., online marketplaces) where the two sides of the market can meet and they charge fees to both or (more usually) one group of users. The reduction in transaction costs (both fixed and marginal) allowed by these platforms and the enlargement of the potential market through their networks have allowed a growing number of firms to offer their products thereby increasing customer choice.

A.1.1.3 Importance of Data

ICT continuously drives down the cost of collecting, storing and analysing data following Moore's law. This has helped to reduce transaction costs, many of which are information related, making many more market transactions possible than previously.

ICT has also driven down costs for consumers in terms of price and choice via the emergence of competing online marketplaces offering a wide range of products. Consumer behaviour—web clicks, online purchases, search engine entries, peer reviews of products and so on—has contributed to the accumulation of vast amounts of data, referred to as Big Data, which offers additional possibilities in an increasingly digitalized economy. Online platform providers process and analyse Big Data to find meaningful correlations in order to specifically target products and services to individual consumers.

Furthermore, Big Data has helped digital firms develop innovative goods and services, with lower costs associated with innovation, in terms of measurement, experimentation, sharing and replication than in the pre-digital age. It is now possible to measure and analyse phenomena to an extent never imaginable before, thus making it easier to run controlled experiments and measure their success with great precision. Digitalization enables companies to run hundreds of controlled experiments every day. An innovation can then be shared easily and developed further within an organization or community—and quickly replicated on a vast scale. Digitalization enables enterprises to increase competitiveness by meeting individual customer needs more accurately and by optimising value chains.

A.2 Defining and Measuring the Digital Economy

Digitalization has emerged in recent years as a key economic driver that accelerates growth, transformation and value creation. It is evident that digitalization has had a dramatic effect on the economy as a whole, and it is likely that this tendency will accelerate in the future. However, attempts to measure the impact have proven problematic.

Booz & Company's econometric analysis estimates that, despite the unfavourable global economic climate, digitization created a 193 billion USD boost to world economic output and created 6 million jobs globally in 2011. On the macro side, Van Ark et al. (2014) calculated that 64% of the growth in labour productivity in the USA between 1995 and 2007 was led by ICT (and complementary) investments. The equivalent contribution in the EU-15 was only 57% and for a much lower total (Table A.1 and Fig. A.1).

The analysis referred to above by Booz & Company reveals that an increase of 10% in a country's digitalization score fuels a 0.75% growth in its GDP per capita. Creating digital markets and boosting digitaliza-

Table A.1 Comparison of EU and US ICT growth impacts (1995–2007)

	EU15	US
GDP growth	2.2	3.1
Labour productivity growth	1.3	2.0
Contributions to labour productivity growth		
IT investment/hour	0.4	0.7
Multi-Factor productivity from ICT production	0.3	0.5
Multi-Factor productivity from ICT use	0.1	0.1
% points IT contribution to labour productivity growth	0.7	1.3
Total IT as % labour productivity growth	57%	64%
Total IT as % of GDP growth	34%	41%

Source: Van Ark et al. (2013)

Syverson (2013) computed labour productivity growth during the electrification era and the IT era (Figure 2) with an impressively similar pattern

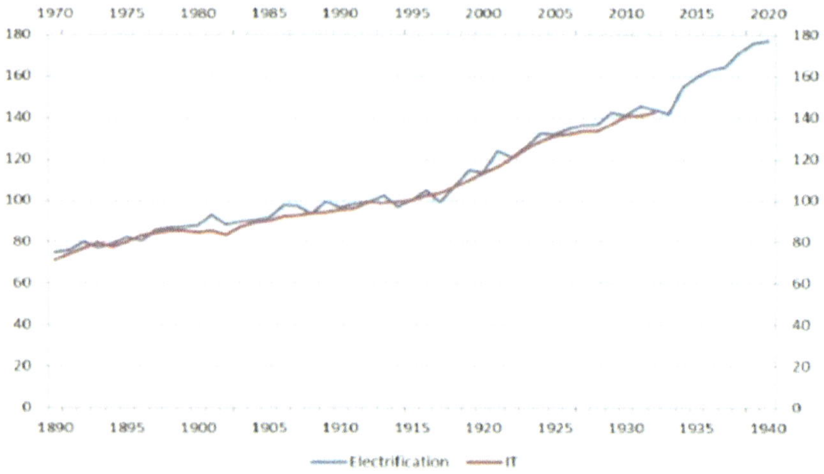

Fig. A.1 Labour productivity growth during the electrification era (1890–1940) and the IT era (1970–2012) in the USA (1915 = 100 and 1995 = 100) (Source: Calculations based on Kendrick (1961) and US Bureau of Statistics data)

tion can yield significant economic benefits and lead to substantial social benefits to societies and communities. Digitalization has the potential to boost productivity and enhance competitiveness. In the current economic environment digitalization can play an important role in assisting policy-makers to enhance competitiveness and spur economic growth and employment.

A.3 Trends in the Digital Economy

ICT-driven innovations which affect the whole economy will exert a further competitive pressure on businesses which will be forced to invest in knowledge. A strategy based on cost reduction will not survive in markets based on innovation. A global reach will be necessary for products displaying both very low marginal costs and network effects. Increasingly, micro-multinationals will come to the fore, particularly in terms of job creation.

Emerging trends in ICT will increase the move towards this model by promoting greater use of technology at the expense of other factors of production. Cloud technology, 3D printing and the Internet of Things will reduce fixed capital investment costs of starting a business—lowering barriers to market access. Conversely, technologies such as advanced robotics, autonomous vehicles and automation of knowledge work (by expert systems) will have a profound impact as many jobs will be replaced by machines.

Digital entrepreneurs and key specialists in the emerging business models will be critical in the future workforce. This will require a mix of entrepreneurial, creative, problem-solving and specialist skills. Work patterns and job contracts will change: the traditional working model is likely to be replaced by flexible working patterns adapted to the needs of the business; remuneration may be more correlated to the fortunes of the enterprise and careers may well involve shorter periods in a given company than in the past.

A.4 Digital Challenges for the EU

The completion of the Single Market—and the Digital Single Market (DSM) in particular—will be key to enabling job and value creation. To maximize the benefits that can be derived from a DSM, existing barriers must be overcome and it is essential that no new fiscal barriers are raised to companies wishing to exploit the huge opportunities open to them. Factors limiting the capacity of the EU to create and attract new companies, such as digital start-ups, include:

- A lack of entrepreneurship and of entrepreneurial culture: Indeed, there is evidence that Europe lacks entrepreneurial skills to move new research results.
- A lack of an appropriately skilled workforce, which calls for a new education strategy for preparing young generations for the skills needed in the digital age and a training strategy to upskill those already in the workforce and those involuntarily unemployed.

- A lack of access to finance: Venture Capital finance (and Business Angel financing which is found extensively in digital start-ups) is scarce and fragmented.
- A rigid labour market: Micro-multinationals need only very few people to run efficiently and they must be able to draw on the best talent. Hence, rigid labour markets may create barriers.

These topics clearly go beyond the mandate of the Group, but are nevertheless critical in order for the EU to be able to leverage the digital opportunity.

A.5 International Taxation in the Digital Economy

In this chapter we identify relevant guiding principles for international taxation that underpin our analysis of policy options. We then describe the relevant business models in the digital economy and their implications for value added tax (VAT) and corporation tax. Finally, we describe the current international debate about taxation and the digital economy.

A.5.1 Principles of Taxation

We focus on three guiding principles for international taxation: (1) economic efficiency, (2) distributional equity and (3) efficiency and effectiveness in compliance and administration. Most taxes affect the behaviour of economic agents—individuals and businesses. A starting point in identifying a good tax system is one that minimizes these effects on behaviour—such a tax generally results in "production efficiency". This is an important starting benchmark for the design of international tax systems. Not all distortions to behaviour harm the economy; in principle, governments could use the tax system to encourage activities that create value for society (such as expenditure on R&D), or to discourage activities that harm society (such as polluting activities). But, in the absence of a clearly defined and well-specified goal, distortions result in a cost to society.

Some effect on economic activity is inevitable in any tax system; but the costs created by taxes depend on the design of the tax. Some forms of taxation create minimal distortions. For example, a tax on the economic rent earned on an investment should, in principle, not affect the scale of the investment. Nevertheless, even such a tax will affect location decisions if the proportion of economic rent taken in tax differs between locations.

A.5.2 Economic Efficiency in an International Setting

In an international setting, two broad types of distortion give rise to departures from production efficiency that arise in addition to those in a domestic setting: firstly, the international location of economic activity or income and secondly, the differential treatment of competing agents. Any such distortions to competition imply deviations from efficiency in production.

The effects of taxation on the location of economic activity depend on the mobility of economic agents, capital, goods and services. The more mobile such factors, the more probable it is that differences in taxation between locations may affect location choices. At one extreme, natural resources are immobile. At the other, the location in which intangible assets are owned can be very mobile. This suggests that to minimize distortions to the location of economic activity taxes on income or spending should be levied in locations in which that income or spending is relatively immobile. For example, consider the taxation of income of an individual who saves in financial assets in many countries. Leaving aside tax administration and compliance, a tax on worldwide income from her savings levied in her residence country should have no effect on where she saves; the tax can only be escaped if she decides to move to another country. By contrast, a tax levied in the location in which she saves is likely to affect her choice of where to save.

Taxes can also affect where real economic activity occurs and even where income is declared for the purposes of taxation. Multinational companies, under existing national and international tax rules can shift profit—and hence tax revenue—between countries. Such profit shifting is considered to be particularly widespread in the case of companies making intensive use of digital technologies in their international activities. While digital companies may be more extreme in this regard, these issues also arise elsewhere.

The second type of distortion arising at an international level is a distortion to competition between businesses. We illustrate competition between businesses with an example. Suppose two similar companies, X and Y, are resident in two different countries and compete with each other in a third country Z. The competition may involve selling similar products to final consumers in Z, or, say, acquiring a particular target company in Z. If X and Y are subject to tax at different rates in their residence countries, then competition may be distorted. For example, a tax advantage to X may enable X to undercut Y's price in selling to a final consumer, or allow X to pay a higher price for the target company. By contrast, if tax were levied only in country Z, then both countries would face the same tax rate on their activities in Z and these distortions to competition would be avoided.

A different form of competition is tax competition between governments as they attempt to attract either economic activity or related tax revenue. Nominal corporation tax rates over the last 30 years in the EU and elsewhere have dropped significantly; for example, across 28 countries in the OECD or G20, the average rate fell from around 47% in 1983 to around 27% in 2012. It is generally agreed that one important factor in this gradual decline is competition between governments for economic activity and related tax revenue. However, tax competition may also take a more invidious form, such as more generous treatment of foreign source income, or of income related to mobile income generators such as the ownership of capital and intellectual property (IP) that is unrelated to real economic activity. While such tax competition seems very likely to have reduced aggregate corporation tax revenue, it may have benefited those jurisdictions competing unfairly for mobile economic activities. Unless there is enforceable international regulation or coordination, unfair tax competition seems inevitable in an international tax system in which the location where corporation tax is levied is based in relatively mobile income generators.

By contrast, there has been little evidence of tax competition between member states due to VAT rate differentials. A fundamental reason is that VAT is generally levied in the country of the consumer. Since the place of taxation generally cannot be influenced by the enterprise, there is no point in governments competing over VAT rates in order to attract internationally mobile business activities. A lower VAT rate in one country has an effect on the welfare of a neighbouring country only in relation to cases of cross-border shopping, which may limit the VAT rate differential between neighbouring member states. Beyond this, VAT rates within the EU are already subject to some form of harmonization. However, in the area of electronically supplied services, distortions of competition have been reported in Business to Consumer (B2C) transactions which should in principle disappear in 2015 when the new rules on the place of supply of telecommunications, broadcasting and electronic services will generalize the place of supply at the place of the consumer.

A.5.3 Distributional Equity

It is vital that tax systems should be fair, and should be seen to be fair. This fairness has two dimensions—sharing tax revenues between countries and sharing the cost of tax among individuals. Since this report concerns distributional equity in an international setting, however, it does not address the latter. This is justified under the assumption that equity across people is dealt with at national level.

The distribution of tax revenues between countries from taxes levied on international flows of goods, services, capital and labour has been the subject of considerable debate and to some extent has driven concerns about the taxation of the digital economy. It has been argued that countries should be entitled to tax income originating within their borders, because it is the "place of income-originating activity." However, this begs the question of what such an activity is. Although it could easily incorporate, say, production as well as sales, it must be remembered that the entire revenue from indirect taxation typically accrues entirely to the place of consumption, thereby allocating a significant share of aggregate tax revenue on cross-border transactions to the countries where the sales take place.

It has also been argued that under a principle of "inter-nation equity" each country should be allocated an equitable share of the tax base from cross-border transactions. However, it is not easy to define what is an equitable allocation of, for example, the profits of a multinational group that operates in many producing and consuming countries. But a result in which some enterprises succeed in avoiding tax on a substantial part of their global income is generally regarded as unfair. In a world in which countries have different interests, a stable international tax system requires the consent of different countries, and an essential element of that is that it should be regarded as providing a fair distribution of revenues.

A.5.4 Compliance and Administration

The costs of administration and compliance are a necessary feature of taxes. It is clearly a reasonable aim for a tax system that such costs should be kept to a minimum, whether the tax is domestic or international. The costs of complying with, and administering, international elements of tax, such as VAT and corporation tax, are particularly high, as both tax payers and tax authorities typically need to take into account international flows and rules. In some circumstances, the administrative costs of collecting tax may be smaller if they are borne by the tax authority of one country even though the revenues accrue to another country. Clearly, such a degree of cooperation between tax authorities in different countries necessarily requires mutual trust and respect.

Administrative and compliance costs depend on the methods used by tax authorities in implementing a tax, but they also depend on policy choices in the design of a tax. An example of the importance of policy choices is where a tax treats two similar activities in different ways. Where this happens, taxpayers will have an incentive to choose the more lightly taxed approach, and tax authorities need to police the borderline between them. A classic example is the tax advantage to debt finance over equity finance in corporation taxes. Such distinctions can create substantial administrative and compliance costs, as taxpayers, tax authorities and the courts attempt to distinguish between very similar contracts. These costs can be important in a domestic context, but they are likely to multiply in an international context as the choice of financial instrument may become a vehicle for tax planning.

Two other issues are also important from the perspective of administration. The first is fairness in the administration of taxes; taxpayers should be treated alike. The second is transparency; taxpayers should be able to have a reasonable understanding of how the tax system operates. This could be taken further; in principle, transparency should extend to a reasonable level of stability—taxpayers should be reasonably certain how the tax system will operate in the future. Even apart from the normative case that taxes should be fair and transparent, lack of either is likely to lead to greater economic inefficiency.

A.6 Business Models in the Digital Economy

A.6.1 Description of Relevant Digital Business Models

In considering how VAT and corporation tax should be applied in an international digital economy, it is useful to describe the typical business models that are applied in the digital economy. We distinguish three separate models set out below. In these models, we distinguish two types of locations:

D—the Destination countries: the places where the final goods are consumed.

S—the Source countries: they comprise the set of different locations of the activities of the business. This includes marketing, sales, distribution, support, R&D, production, financing, management and other locations where the business owns assets and/or operates. There are two more important locations, but they are not distinct in the different business models:

P—the Parent country: where the parent company is resident and usually the location of the headquarter activities of the business.

F—the Financing country or countries: the place of residence of individuals and companies who provide finance to the business, either as shareholders or debt holders.

1. Physical e-commerce models

This first model is the traditional e-commerce business model from the "physical" world. A physical product is made in S and sold online to a customer in D. Because the product is physical, the location of sales, distribution and support is typically in the same country as the customer, i.e., also in D, even though it may have been produced elsewhere.

2. Digital e-commerce and cloud models (product or service delivered digitally)

In the second model, the "product" is not physical but digital. It is either distributed over the web as a product or it is kept at a central data centre and distributed as a service. For the digital e-commerce models, the main difference compared to the physical model is that a digital product can be distributed and supported from locations that are very distant from D. Similarly, for cloud services consumers access the central data centre from a location of their choosing (D), but the central data centre itself can be located in any S country provided there is Internet access.

Moreover, several customers can consume the same "product" at the same time (public cloud service), so the marginal cost of gaining additional customers is low. In model 2, the digital nature of the transaction—whether product or service—makes the S countries largely independent from the location of customers in the D country. Examples of these models are downloading in return for a fee or online streaming services in return for a fee.

3. Multidimensional models

The third model combines two or more dimensions. The first concerns a free digital service for a group of users in country D1. This dimension generates value by selling advertising seen by users in D1 within a second dimension possibly located in another country, D2. In the first dimension also typically data are collected from the users in D1 which allows the advertisements to be better targeted. The irrelevance of location is even more pronounced in the multidimensional model: the physical location of users in the first dimension can be different to the physical location of business customers in the second. Moreover, both are independent of S, the location of the service provider. Examples of these multidimensional business models include search engines, social networks or other free digital service websites combined with advertising business.

A.6.2 Digital Business Models and their Tax Implications

The different locations where business activities take place are relevant in determining where VAT and corporation tax are to be levied. The fact that VAT is generally thought of as a tax on consumption and is even defined as such in Article 1(2) of the VAT Directive implies that it should reasonably be levied in country D—the destination country. If the tax is levied in D, then the location of the activities of the business are not relevant for VAT. Consequently, in choosing the set of source locations the business will not be affected by the tax. Furthermore, if the tax is levied in D, businesses competing with each other to sell to consumers in D will all face the same rate of VAT thus avoiding distortion of competition. Therefore, it is reasonable to continue to implement VAT on sales of goods and services in the destination country. From 2015, in the EU sales of digital products to final consumers in country D will be subject to VAT in country D.

Corporation tax is broadly a tax on corporate revenues, net of costs of labour, capital consumption/depreciation and other inputs. Under existing international tax standards, corporation tax is broadly levied in the set of "source" countries, S, in each of which the parent company P will have incorporated a separate subsidiary company. Tax may in some circumstances be levied in country P25, and indeed D, although only if there is a permanent establishment (PE) there. Corporation tax being levied in S is sometimes justified on the grounds that it can be seen as a form of "benefit" tax; the business uses publicly provided goods and services in countries in which it operates, and it should make a contribution to their costs through taxation.

In the multidimensional business model above, the business typically extracts information from users in D1 and uses this information to target advertisers in D2. The business provides the free use of its service such as a search engine or social network and "in exchange" the user provides the information. This is, in effect, a barter arrangement. It is not obvious that the business creates any profit in the first dimension, and even if it does, it monetizes it in the second dimension.

Allocation of profit across the different source locations puts pressure on the proper functioning of international corporation tax systems. These challenges are made more difficult by the key features of the digital economy described in Sect. A.1.1: mobility, network effects and data. They relate to how digital businesses create value initially and subsequently generate revenues from this value. Combined, they impact on the application of traditional methods to allocate profits from international business operations to the activities and functions that have generated the profits. Addressing these challenges is part of the wider international debate about whether international (digital) corporations pay their fair share of tax within the combined project of the G20/OECD Project on base erosion and profit shifting.

A.7 The G20/OECD "BEPS" Project

A.7.1 BEPS General

Following a series of press publications and parliamentary hearings, the international community led by the G20 has initiated a project on Base Erosion and Profit Shifting (BEPS). The fundamental idea behind the project is that national and international corporation tax laws and standards may not have kept pace with the way global corporations run their business. As a result the locations to which taxable profits are allocated for corporation tax purposes differ from those where the actual business activity takes place. It is that discrepancy, as well as problems in identifying where relevant business activities take place, which the project aims to address.

The OECD BEPS Action Plan lists separate actions. They are organized as separate elements that address the overall politically undesirable BEPS effects, for example excessive deduction of interest, harmful tax competition, treaty shopping or transfer pricing aspects related to intangibles. The G20/OECD BEPS Project primarily concerns corporation tax; nevertheless, there are also significant issues related to VAT in particular in relation to the digital economy.

A.7.2 BEPS and the Digital Economy

Many of the high-profile cases that have caused the public anxiety driving the political G20 BEPS agenda concern digital companies. There is a perception, supported by some of the publicly available data, that BEPS is especially prevalent in the digital economy. Annex 2A and 2B provide an overview of the corporation tax charge in relation to income and sales for a sample of the largest digital and non-digital companies. They all concern US multinationals because the data published under US public financial reporting rules are the only publicly available tax data that allow such comparison. The data demonstrate that both samples of companies generally pay more tax on their US-based earnings than on their non-US source earnings, but the difference is more pronounced for digital companies than for non-digital. This difference and the prominence of digital economy related enterprises in discussions related to tax planning and BEPS, particularly in the EU, can be explained by a combination of elements:

- Digital companies are young and dynamic

Even the largest digital firms are young enterprises. This has allowed them from the outset to structure their business in a tax optimized form, often locating the group's entities and its IP in locations with low corporation tax or VAT rates and/or with access to favourable double tax conventions. Mature companies often need to engage in costly and burdensome restructuring to achieve similar results involving legal and financial risk, which often causes internal resistance.

- Digital companies rarely pay out dividends

Not paying dividends leads to tax advantages. Many of the digital global giants are US companies. In the US tax system, foreign profits are not subject to US taxation until they are distributed. Not paying dividends to shareholders means there is no need to repatriate cash from foreign operations, thus effectively allowing the deferral of taxation on foreign profits. In theory this is a temporary deferral, but in practice almost permanent deferral seems to be the rule rather than the exception.

- Mobility: absence of physical presence in the market and mobility of profit drivers (IP)

Important business functions in digital companies take place on the Web. As a result, they do not need a distinct physical presence in the markets in which they operate. This allows digital businesses to avoid creating a taxable presence in these markets. At the same time, some of the current international tax standards allow them to allocate a significant part of their global revenues to their internally developed IP and to locate this IP for tax purposes in locations that do not impose taxation.

- The nature of successful businesses in the digital economy

Several digital economy business/revenue models have been extremely successful in rapidly developing monopoly-like positions and in rapidly generating significant revenues from the collection, processing and marketing of free individual data. In other words, the digital economy includes some extremely successful businesses that have generated enormous wealth in a short time frame. This makes the application of BEPS schemes correspondingly more beneficial for digital companies.

The Actions listed in the OECD BEPS Action Plan will to a large extent help to address these concerns. Nevertheless, the G20/OECD considers that the specifics of the digital economy including indirect tax issues merit listing the digital economy as a separate Action item number 1 in the OECD BEPS Action Plan.

Bibliography

"About Us". (2005–2011). The streamlined sales tax governing board. http://www.streamlinedsalestax.org/index.php?page=About-Us

Adonnino, P. 1 commercio via Internet e la fiscalità: gli aspetti generali delle attività transnazionali e nazionali. In R. Rinaldi (Ed.), *La fiscalità del commercio via Internet: attualità e prospettive*. Giappichelli.

"Building the European Information Society for Us All: Final Policy Report of the High-Level Expert Group". (1997). Archive of Europena Integration (AEI). http://aei.pitt.edu/8692/

Cerina, P. (2003). II problema della legge applicabile. In E. Tosi (Ed.), *I problemi giuridici di Internet. Dall'e-commerce all'e-business*. Milan: Giuffré.

Cipollina, S. (2003). *I confini giuridici del tempo presente. Il caso del diritto fiscal.* Milano: Giuffrè.

Commission Expert Group on Taxation of the Digital Economy. (2014, May). "Annex 3" in report. http://ec.europa.eu/taxation_customs/resources/documents/taxation/gen_info/good_governance_matters/digital/report_digital_economy.pdf

Corte Costituzionale. (1973, July 16). No. 131.

Corte Costituzionale. (1979, July 26). No. 89.

F. Boccia, R. Leonardi (eds.), *The Challenge of the Digital Economy*,
DOI 10.1007/978-3-319-43690-6

Costanzo, P. (2000). Internet (diritto pubblico). In *Digesto (disc. pubb.)*. (vol. I). UTET.

De Rosa, V. (2003). La formazione di regole giuridiche per il “cyberspazio”. In Riv. Inf. e informatica.

Donald, B., William, F., & LeAnn, L. (2009). *State and local government sales tax revenue losses from electronic commerce*. Knoxville: University of Tennessee.

Empiris LLC, Eisenach, J.A., & Litan, R.E. Uncollected sales tax on electronic commerce: A reality check. http://netchoice.org/wp-content/uploads/eisenach-litan-state-estimates.pdf

Ficari, V. (2003). Regime fiscale delle transazioni telematiche. In Rassegna Tributaria.

Gall, M. B., & Kulwicki, L. A. (2012). *A lawmaker's guide to sales tax Nexus*. Milwaukee: University of Wisconsin-Milwaukee, Sheldon B. Lubar School of Business.

Gilmore III, J. S. *No internet tax: A proposal submitted to the policies & options paper of the advisory commission on electronic commerce*. http://www.ecommercecommission.org

Henchman, J. (2012, August 1). *Written submission of Joseph Henchman – Hearing on marketplace fairness: Leveling the playing field for small businesses before the committee on commerce, science, and transportation U.S. Senate*. http://taxfoundation.org/article/written-submission-joseph-henchman-hearing-marketplace-fairness-leveling-playing-field-small

Henchman, J., & Borean, R. (2014, March). *State sales tax jurisdictions approach 10,000*. Tax Foundation. http://taxfoundation.org/blog/state-sales-tax-jurisdictions-approach-10000

Huenink, D. (2013). Eliminating the e-commerce sales tax advantage in the United States by following in the footsteps of the European Union. *Wisconsin International Law Journal, 31*(1), 65–89.

Inzitari, B. (2001). Contratti su Internet: aspetti della dematerializzazione. In R. Rinaldi (Ed.), *La fiscalità del commercio via Internet: attualità e prospettive*. Torino: Giappichelli.

Irti, N. (2002). Norma e luoghi. Problemi di geo diritto (Cacucci).

Kocieniewski, D. (2011, March 25–December 30). But nobody pays that. *New York Times*. Accessed at http://topics.nytimes.com/top/features/timestopics/series/but_nobody_pays_that/index.html

Mastroiacovo, V. (2004). Il controllo, l'accertamento e la riscossione dei crediti tributari derivanti da transazioni telematiche. In *Riv.dir.trib.* (vol. I).

McFarland, C., & Pagano, M. A. (2015). *City fiscal conditions in 2015*. Washington, DC: National League of Cities.

Meijers, H. (2014). Does the internet generate economic growth, international trade, or both? *International Economics and Economic Policy, 11*, 137–163.

Mullins, D. R., & Joyce, P. G. (1996). Tax and expenditure limitations and state and local fiscal structure: An empirical assessment. *Public Budgeting & Finance, 16*(1), 75–101.

Mullins, D. R., & Wallin, B. A. (2004). Tax and expenditure limitations: Introduction and overview. *Public Budgeting & Finance, 24*(4), 2–15.

National Bellas Hess v. Illinois Department of Revenue. (1967). 386 U.S. 753.

OECD. (2011, September 28). ICTNET assessment paper 1, ICT growth and productivity. Accessed at https://community.oecd.org/docs/DOC-31372

OECD. (2013). *Addressing base erosion and profit shifting*. OECD Publishing. http://dx.doi. org/10.1787/9789264192744-en

Pagano, M. A. (2010). Creative designs of the patchwork quilt of municipal finance. In G. K. Ingram & H. Yu-Hung (Eds.), *The changing landscape of local public revenues*. Cambridge, MA: Lincoln Institute of Land Policy.

Quill Corp. v. North Dakota. (1992). 504 U.S. 298.

Rifkin, J. (2001). *The age of access: The new culture of hypercapitalism, where all of life is a paid-for experience*. New York: Penguin.

Roccatagliata, F., & Valente, P. (1999). Bit tax: ultima frontiera nella società dell'informazione? In il fFiscoisco.

"UK Government tax receipts since 1963". (2013, March 18). Simon Rogers. *The Guardian*. https://www.theguardian.com/news/datablog/2010/apr/25/tax-receipts-1963

UKTI, Inward Investment Report 2014–2015. (2015, June). https://www.gov.uk/government/publications/ukti-inward-investment-report-2014-to-2015

US Census Bureau, Government Organization Summary Report. (2012). http://www2.census.gov/govs/cog/g12_org.pdf. Accessed 22 Jan 2016.

"Use Tax Collection on Income Tax Returns in Other States". (2012, April). Policy brief, research department, Minnesota house of representatives.

Van Ark, B., O'Mahony, M., & Timmer, M. (2008). The productivity gap between Europe and the United States. *Journal of Economic Perspectives, 22*(1), 25–44.

Index[1]

[1] Note: Pagenumbers followed by "n" refers to notes.

F. Boccia, R. Leonardi (eds.), *The Challenge of the Digital Economy*,
DOI 10.1007/978-3-319-43690-6

G

H

I

U

The manufacturer's authorised representative in the EU is Springer Nature Customer Service Centre GmbH, Europaplatz 3, 69115 Heidelberg, Germany. If you have any concerns regarding our products, please contact ProductSafety@springernature.com

Printed and bound by CPI Group (UK) Ltd, Croydon, CR0 4YY
30/09/2026
02225472-0010